A Christmas SLEIGH RIDE

A Double Delight of
Nostalgia in Two Romances

Tracey V. BATEMAN • *Jill* STENGL

BARBOUR
PUBLISHING

© 2004 *Colder Than Ice* by Jill Stengl
© 2004 *Take Me Home* by Tracey V. Bateman

ISBN 1-59310-420-0

Published by Barbour Publishing, Inc., P.O. Box 719, Uhrichsville, Ohio 44683, www.barbourbooks.com

Our mission is to publish and distribute inspirational products offering exceptional value and biblical encouragement to the masses.

 Member of the
Evangelical Christian
Publishers Association

Printed in the United States of America.
5 4 3 2 1

A Christmas
SLEIGH RIDE

Colder Than Ice

by Jill Stengl

Dedication

With love to my daughter and toughest writing critic,
Anne Elisabeth Stengl, and to my sister, Paula Ciccotti,
who introduced me to prairie life in Iowa.

Chapter 1

Coon's Hollow, Iowa—1885

Hello! Sir, hello!"

As Frank Nelson jogged his horse past the Coon's Hollow train station, he noticed a strange woman waving a handkerchief from the sun-baked platform. At first he thought she must be beckoning to someone else, but a quick glance around ended that hope. "Ma'am?" He reined Powder in and halted near the steps.

Clad in black from her bonnet to her boots, the woman twisted the handkerchief between her gloved hands. A large trunk waited beside the empty depot office, and two carpetbags sat on the bench. "I'm sorry to disturb you, sir, but can you deliver a message for me?"

"Deliver it where?" After a sleepless night, he was in no mood to serve as messenger boy. He squinted, thinking she looked vaguely familiar. "Who are you?"

She drew herself up and stared at him down her long, narrow nose. Hot, gusty wind sent her bonnet flapping around her gaunt cheeks and ballooned her ruffled skirts. Soot streaked her forehead, and dust grayed her garments. "If you would ask someone from the hotel to collect my luggage, I shall be grateful."

That incisive voice rang a bell. "Have we met?"

"Never."

Squinting against the wind, he studied her face. Shadowed eyes, sharp chin, and prominent cheekbones. "Are you related to Paul Truman?" Certainty filled him. "You must be his sister from Wisconsin. What are you doing here?"

"I cannot see that it is your business," she began, then informed him, "I have been offered employment in the area."

"That was months ago."

"And how would you know?" Queen Victoria herself could be no more imperious.

"I'm Frank Nelson, the pastor. I offered you the job, Miss Truman. I hope you at least informed Paul and

Susan that you were coming."

"*You* are the minister?" Chin tucked, she looked him up and down. Her shoulders squared. "Has the position been filled?"

"No."

He was tempted to tell her he no longer needed a secretary. Let the harpy go back to the big city and terrorize small children there. Coon's Hollow held its quota of odd characters. And he definitely didn't need another eccentric spinster in his life.

"Why don't you come with me to the parsonage, cool off in the shade, and have some lemonade, and I'll send someone to Trumans' with a message from you. It's only going to get hotter on that platform." His shepherd calling wouldn't allow him to leave even an ornery ewe to the mercy of the elements. She would be in no danger from wolves, that was certain.

She blinked. "Very well."

Frank dismounted, leaped up the steps, and grabbed her carpetbags. "They're planning a new depot with a covered waiting area, but it won't happen this year. Have you been here long?" *She must have arrived on the morning train.*

"What about my trunk?"

"It'll be safe here until Paul comes for it. The parsonage is just around the corner." He hopped down and swung the two bags up onto Powder's saddle. When he turned around, Miss Truman had descended the steps. She was tall, he noticed. And thin. Truly spindly.

"Miss Truman?" He extended his arm. She curled her gloved fingers around his forearm and fell into step along the dusty street. Powder followed behind, led by one loose rein. Now that Frank had offered lemonade, he remembered drinking the last of it yesterday afternoon.

He tried to recall details about Miss Truman. Upon hearing of their mother's death, Paul had offered his only sister a home with his family, adding the further incentive of a job as the minister's secretary. "Taking her into my home is the Christian thing to do," Paul had said with the air of a martyr. "And she could be a great help to you if she doesn't drive you to an early grave."

Frank gave the woman a side glance. She appeared more underfed and exhausted than dangerous. "Why did you decide to come to Iowa after all? When Paul had no reply from you, he assumed you weren't coming."

"My circumstances became. . .insupportable," she said in a flat voice. "If you no longer require my services, I shall find employment elsewhere."

"What did Paul tell you about me?" He felt awkward asking.

"He told me that you are attempting to write a book

and need someone to transcribe it for you. Is your office in your home or at the church?"

"At the parsonage."

"I assume your wife will act as chaperone."

As if this woman would require one. "My housekeeper will chaperone; my wife died eight years ago."

"You have no family?"

"Not living with me. My daughter, Amy, is married and living in Des Moines. My son, David, recently bought a farm near your brother's and is fixing up the farmhouse. He is betrothed to your niece, Margie. They are to marry Christmas Eve, so you and I shall soon be related in a way."

"I see."

"Here we are." Frank wrapped Powder's rein around the post and pushed open the picket gate. Seeing Miss Truman examine his home, he scanned it himself. A riot of perennials overflowed the garden fence, invaded the weedy lawn, and sneaked across the walkway. Morning glories strangled the hitching posts and attempted to bind the picket gate shut.

A wide veranda wrapped around most of the house, offering shade and a breeze. Beyond the stable out back, cornfields stretched as far as the eye could see. A windmill squeaked out its rusty rhythm. Water trickled from its base into a huge tub. A swaybacked horse plunged its nose into the sparkling water and playfully dumped waves over the tub's far rim.

"The Harlan Coon family donated this house and the stable to the church twenty years ago. Those are Coon cornfields, but Bess there is mine. She's too old to work, but I keep her as company for Powder." A handy excuse for keeping an oversized pet. "The church is a good stretch of the legs up the road from here, but the walk gives me exercise."

The woman said nothing. These long silences seemed uncanny from a female. Perhaps she was tired. "Have a seat here, Miss Truman, and I'll find you something to drink. Mary should be around somewhere." It occurred to him that the simplest course of action would be to hitch up his own buggy and take the lady to Paul's house.

The screen door squealed, and Mary Bilge stumped onto the porch. An unlit cigar dangled from her lips. "Who's this?"

"Miss Truman, newly arrived from Wisconsin. Miss Truman, this is Miss Bilge, my housekeeper." He watched the two women eye each other and shake hands. "Miss Truman has agreed to assist me with preparing my manuscript for publication."

Mary's dark gaze pinned him. "How's the Dixons' baby?"

"Better, the doctor says."

"Humph. I'll bake them a raisin loaf."

He would believe that when he saw it. "Uh, do we have any of that lemonade left, Mary?"

"You oughta know, seein' as how you drank the last of it." She disappeared back into the house, letting the screen door slam.

Frank avoided Miss Truman's gaze. "I'm sorry."

"May I enter your kitchen?"

"Certainly." He opened the screen door and beckoned her inside. She peeled off her gloves, surveying the room, the largest in his house. To his surprise, she opened the firebox and added two sticks of wood, picked up the kettle, and nodded. "I can make tea, if you have any."

"Help yourself. I don't know what I have. People give me food sometimes. Like the lemonade Mrs. Wilkins brought over."

Miss Truman searched through cupboards, canisters, and the icebox, producing a tin of tea, a sack of white sugar, and a small pitcher of cream. Frank watched her brew tea in an old china teapot. Whenever she glanced his way, he found himself standing straight and holding in his gut.

"You may summon Miss Bilge." The lady located cookies in the jar and laid them on a plate, loaded the waiting tray, and carried it out to the porch before Frank could stop her.

"Come and have tea on the veranda with us, Mary," he called, uncertain where she might be. "Then I need to hitch up Powder and take Miss Truman home."

He heard Mary thumping and muttering on the cellar stairs. What had she been doing down there? He didn't dare ask.

"Tea on a day like this? La-de-da! Give me coffee."

"But Miss Truman brewed tea."

"Coffee's good enough for me. Got some left from breakfast."

Frank grimaced at the idea, but Mary poured herself a cup and shuffled outside. In hot or cold weather, she always wore the same man's overcoat over a sacklike gown, heavy boots, and a broad-brimmed hat. She seemed about as wide as she was tall. Slumped into a rocking chair, she seared Miss Truman with her stare.

Serenely composed, Miss Truman perched in another chair, prepared to pour the tea. "Cream and sugar, Reverend Nelson?"

"Thank you." After pulling up a third rocking chair, he watched her prepare his tea and accepted the cup. Her remote gaze caught his once more. "Reverend Nelson, when do you wish me to begin work?"

He sipped the tea. Sweet, creamy—better than he had expected. "How about Monday? That should give you time to settle in at Paul and Susan's. I warn you, my papers are a disaster."

"Huh," Mary said, cradling her grimy coffee cup against her chest.

Frank started to grin but stopped when his lips quivered. He took a handful of cookies.

Silence lengthened. Frank wondered if the women could hear him chewing. No telling how long those cookies had been in the jar. Since spring maybe.

A large black cat strolled across the veranda, gave Mary wide berth, oozed between Frank's boots, and sat in front of Miss Truman. The lady moved her teacup to one side, and the cat flowed into her lap, curled up, and disappeared against the shiny black fabric.

"Dirty critter," Mary muttered.

Miss Truman stroked the cat, and Frank heard a rumbling purr. Again he met Miss Truman's gaze and, for the first time, saw in her pale eyes a fleeting emotion. "I like cats," she said.

Frank gulped down the last of his tea. "We have several roaming about the place. Belle is the queen cat and the best mouser. We used to have a dog, but he died a few years back of old age."

Miss Truman watched the cat as she petted it, and Frank watched her long hands caress its glossy fur. Abruptly she took a sip of tea. The cup rattled in the saucer when she replaced it, and Frank suddenly noticed the slump of her shoulders. The poor woman must be exhausted almost beyond bearing, yet he'd kept her drinking tea on his veranda and talking business. He hopped up, leaving his chair rocking wildly. "We'd best be off, Miss Truman. If you'd like to rest awhile longer, I'll take the buckboard to the station for your trunk first and return for you."

She nodded. "Thank you, Reverend Nelson." Rising, she gathered up the tea things and carried them inside. The screen door closed quietly behind her.

"You're gonna hire that woman? She's gonna be here every day?" Mary glowered.

"I'm hiring her as secretary, not replacement house-keeper. Your place is secure."

Scowl lines deepened between Mary's brushy brows. With another grunt, she set her empty coffee cup on the floor and rose. Nose high, she stumped down the porch steps and headed toward her little house across the road.

When Frank drove through town with Estelle Truman at his side, he encountered curious glances from townspeople. She shaded her face with a black silk parasol and sat erect on the bench seat. Polished boot toes emerged from beneath her gown's dusty ruffles. For the first time, he noticed the worn seams on her sleeves and a rip in the skirt, repaired with tiny stitches.

"We'll have you home in no time," he promised as they left the schoolhouse and one last barking dog behind. "So, Miss Truman, you have lived in Madison all your life until now?"

"I have. Reverend Nelson, I do not wish to confide my life story in you during this drive to my brother's farmhouse. I'm sure you will understand."

He deflated. "Of course."

"I overheard your conversation with Miss Bilge today—something about the illness of a baby?" She spoke quietly.

"Ben and Althea Dixon's first child. Only nine months old. He took ill last week. The doctor thought he would die, but he rallied during the night and seemed almost back to normal. I was on my way home from their house when I met you at the station."

"Were you with the family all night?"

"Yes. They asked me to come and pray, and this time God chose to restore little Benjamin's health. We lose a lot of children here. Paul and Susan's daughter, Jessamine, died of typhoid a year ago, and they nearly lost Joe, too."

"Paul never wrote of their daughter's death."

"Jessamine was sixteen. I believe the sorrow and strain have drained Susan's strength, yet her spirit is stronger than ever."

Miss Truman's chin tipped up. "I shall not increase Susan's burden. She will find me useful around the house."

"I pray you'll also find time to assist me in preparing my book for publication. I often fear I should abandon the project and turn my mind to more practical pursuits, but then I feel as if God is pressing this work upon my heart and I must keep writing it." He looked down at her marble profile and wondered if she could make any difference.

"I shall assist you to the best of my ability, Reverend Nelson, commensurate with my pay."

Rather than respond to that baffling remark, he pointed. "Ahead is Paul's farm. All this corn around us is his. He also raises hogs. He's a good man. Good farmer. Good friend. I'm honored to have my son marry his daughter." He turned in at the Trumans' drive, wondering how the family would react to this maiden aunt's arrival.

The barn and the white farmhouse looked insignificant in the vast expanse of surrounding prairie. One large tree shaded the house. Chickens ran clucking from the buckboard as it rolled up the drive, and a cow bawled.

Frank glanced at Miss Truman. Her expression revealed nothing.

"Hello, Frank. Who's that with—" The question cut off sharply. Paul jogged across the farmyard, his eyes locked with his sister's. "Estelle!"

"Hello, Paul. I came."

He stopped beside the buckboard, still staring. "I can't believe it."

"If you have changed your mind, I can take a room in town."

He seemed to start back to reality. "No, no. Here, let me help you down." He offered her a hand, and while she climbed to the ground, he turned his head to shout over one shoulder. "Josh. Alvin. Joe. Get out here *now*!

"I just can't believe it. You haven't changed much, Stell." Paul gave her a quick hug.

Frank saw her lips quiver before she stepped back to straighten her bonnet. "Twenty years, Paulie."

One after another, Paul's three sons appeared from barn and fields. Frank saw little Flora poke her head out the kitchen door, then duck back inside, probably to inform her mother about their visitors. Eliza, the farm dog, came running, tail wagging as she sniffed around Miss Truman's shoes. To Frank's surprise, the woman held out one hand to the dog and gave her a pat.

While Paul introduced his sister to the boys, Frank unloaded her trunk and bags from his wagon. She spoke to the boys politely and shook their hands. Frank caught an exchange of uncertain glances between Al and Joe. Josh unobtrusively punched the younger boy when he made a comment behind one hand.

Susan and her daughters emerged from the house, and Frank felt himself relax. A welcoming smile wreathed Susan's face, and her daughters were beaming. "Estelle! This is a wonderful surprise. My dear, please come inside out of this heat. The men will bring your things in. You can share Margie's room until she marries." Amid a spate of further instructions and welcomes, Susan took Miss Truman's hand in hers and led her toward the house. The three boys picked up the luggage and followed.

Paul met Frank's gaze. "I can't believe it," he repeated. "What are we going to do?"

"You invited her here," Frank said. "She came. Susan doesn't seem to mind. Why should you? She's *your* sister."

Paul still looked dazed. "How did you meet her?"

Frank related the scene at the depot. Paul kept shaking his head until Frank wanted to shake him. Miss Truman might be haughty and reserved, but she was no monster. "She agreed to start working for me on Monday, so she won't be around your house all day. I assume you thought of transportation."

"She can use the dogcart."

"She told me she won't be a burden to Susan."

Paul let out a huff. "Don't look at me like that, Frank. You don't understand. Stell and I were good buddies as children. But she changed during the war. When I came home. . .trust me: That woman has a block of ice in place of a heart. I won't let her destroy my home like an encroaching glacier."

"Do you want me to stay around this evening?" Frank offered. "Just for a while?"

"No, thanks. We'll manage." Paul gave Frank a sidelong glance. "But I'd surely appreciate your prayers."

Chapter 2

Without looking in their direction, Frank knew when the Truman family neared his position at the open double doors. He patted an elderly parishioner's hand, gazed into her eyes, and thanked her for her compliments on his sermon. "God's Word is my source, Mrs. Coon. A preacher cannot go far wrong if he sticks to his source. Bless you, ma'am." The widow of the town's founding citizen always had something kind to say.

For two days Frank had been wondering how Miss Truman was adapting to her new surroundings and how her family was adjusting to her. He both dreaded and anticipated introducing her to his dilapidated manuscript on the morrow.

Paul gripped his hand hard. "Good message. Supper

with us this evening? David's already coming."

"Lately it seems the only way I get to see my son is to meet him at your house. Can't imagine why," Frank said, grinning. "Thank you. I'll be there." Anything beat Mary Bilge's Sunday stew. And the fellowship at Paul's house was always excellent.

"Pastor Nelson, thank you for that wonderful sermon." Susan's smile radiated inner beauty. "I always leave this church inspired to live another week in the Lord's presence."

Miss Truman stood nearby, hearing every word. Frank lowered his gaze, cleared his throat, and said, "It's the Holy Ghost, not me."

"I know, but you're His instrument. Come by at five o'clock tonight."

Susan moved on. Margie, Joe, and Flora each shook his hand in turn. Josh and Alvin had passed through the line earlier. Flora asked him, "You met Auntie Stell, didn't you? She likes cats."

He looked into the child's pale blue eyes, then up at her aunt's, noting the resemblance. "I know she does. She met Belle at my house the other day."

"And she is going to make me a blue gown for Margie's wedding."

"Indeed?"

"Today we're going to make pies from the blackberries Joe and I picked yesterday. I get to roll the crust, Auntie Stell says. Margie never lets me. You get to have pie after supper tonight."

"I can hardly wait."

Flora returned his smile and walked on, head high, shoulders back, without her usual bounce. Frank suspected imitation of her aunt, and the realization surprised him.

He turned to face Miss Truman. "I trust you are adjusting to your new home? Flora is evidently smitten with you."

"She is a sweet child." Yet no hint of a smile curved the woman's tight lips. "Thank you for your inquiry, Reverend." After barely touching his hand, she moved on.

Frank shook hands with the last few people, then walked around, straightening hymnals and picking up rubbish. Two calls to make that afternoon, then supper at the Trumans'. These next few weeks should prove interesting in many ways. Perhaps after all these years, he would begin to make headway on his manuscript.

"How are things going with your aunt?" Frank asked Alvin that afternoon as he stabled his gelding in the Trumans' barn.

"Not bad."

Hardly the informative answer Frank desired. "She gets along with your ma?"

"Yep. She's a good cook."

"And your pa doesn't fight with her?" Frank bent to pat Eliza, letting the dog lick his hand.

"Nope. She don't talk much."

A family trait, apparently. "See you at supper."

"Yessir."

Paul greeted him at the front door.

"How are things going?" Frank asked, hanging his hat on the hall tree. He ran his fingers through his damp hair and hoped he didn't stink of sweat and horses.

"Surprisingly well. My sister jumped right into the chores, cooking and cleaning. Even washed and ironed the family's laundry along with her own and started in on the mending. I didn't know she had it in her. Guess she's learned how to work since our childhood days."

Paul led him to the kitchen. "Pastor's here."

Miss Truman and Flora worked over at the counter. Neither one looked up.

"Hello, Dad." David sat at the kitchen table, conversing with Margie while she helped prepare the meal. "Good sermon this morning."

Frank reached across the table to shake his son's hand.

"Thank you. How are things going?"

"Very well. If you have time this week, I could use help replacing the windows in the parlor. The frames are rotted, and two of the panes are cracked. I decided to replace them entirely. It's slow work, but I expect to have the house ready by December." David smiled at Margie, who gazed adoringly into his eyes.

"What about the harvest?"

"Mr. Gallagher put only three fields into corn and beans this year before I bought the place. Harvest should be quick. Got five hogs ready for market by next week. It's a great farm." Enthusiasm burned in David's eyes. Frank recognized himself at that age. So zealous for life, with a promising future and a lovely bride.

When David's attention returned to Margie, Frank allowed himself a look at Miss Truman. Wearing a calico apron over her black mourning gown, she laid a circle of pastry atop a mounded heap of blackberries, all the while chatting with Flora. Her sleeves were rolled up, revealing white arms. Silver laced the waves of dark hair around her forehead.

"Hello, Pastor Nelson." Susan's greeting from the pantry doorway jolted him back to reality. Holding up two jars, she said, "Estelle, I have pickled beets and dilled cucumbers. Which do you think?"

"With chicken pie, I would serve the cucumbers, but this is your home, Susan."

"Nonsense, sister," Susan said. "It's your home now, too. And it's your chicken pie."

"Hello, Susan. I didn't see you there," Frank said. "Can I do anything to help?"

She gave him an odd look. "You needn't shout, Pastor. My hearing is excellent."

Frank felt his face burn. Anxiety sometimes increased his volume.

"If you truly wish to help, you may carry the chicken pie to the table once it's baked." Susan moved toward the work counter.

Frank tried to make himself small to let her pass, but she stepped on his boot. "Excuse me, Pastor."

"Sorry." He shuffled back, colliding with Miss Truman. "Pardon."

Giving an exasperated huff, Miss Truman planted one hand between his shoulder blades and pushed away. He turned to see her brushing flour from her skirts and staring downward. Following her gaze, he beheld his scuffed, cracked brown boot toes emerging beneath striped gray trousers. Did his feet look as large to her as they felt to him?

Without a word, she returned to her pie, and Frank felt himself scorned. "I'd best remove myself from the kitchen before I break something." He laughed and saw Estelle wince. Another loud-mouthed gaffe.

Before he could escape, Flora slid in close and caught his sleeve. "Auntie Stell made an extra pie from my berries for the Dixons 'cause their baby was sick. She made a chicken pie for them, too. Josh took supper to them, but he'll be back before our supper is cooked."

"How thoughtful," Frank said quietly. "I'm certain Althea and Ben will appreciate your kindness."

Flora beamed. Miss Truman did not even glance in his direction. Frank patted Flora's shoulder and tried to smile. He longed to slink away and lick his wounds.

At supper, the men discussed the town baseball team's latest game while Margie chatted about wedding plans with the ladies. Alvin, Joe, and Flora remained politely silent. Needing no urging, Frank accepted a second helping of chicken pie. Its crust flaked over creamy gravy and tender strips of chicken. He wanted to compliment the cook, but her expression discouraged light conversation.

Susan voiced Frank's thoughts. "Estelle, this pie is delicious."

"Where did you learn to cook like this?" Paul asked. "Not at the office of Blackstone and Hicks, I'm certain."

"Our great-aunt Bridget taught me to cook while she lived with us."

Paul chuckled. "Aunt Bridget! I haven't thought about her for decades. Remember the time we brought the litter of raccoons into the parlor while she and Mother were having tea?"

Joe and Alvin stared in silent disbelief.

"We truly did." Paul nodded. "Back in those days, we were a pair of rascals. Most of our pranks were Stell's idea. I was the trusting little brother."

Miss Truman's lips tightened. "Nonsense."

"Aunt Bridget, the ornery old buzzard." Paul leaned back in his chair and reminisced. "We called her 'the witch' when our parents weren't around. She always wore black, and she always looked disapproving. Aunt Bridget taught you more than cooking, Stell."

"She also taught me piano."

"That's not what I meant. You're just like her. I hadn't realized until you mentioned her name; then the resemblance struck me."

Frank heard several sharp gasps around the table. His chest felt tight, but not one beneficial word came to mind.

Miss Truman pushed back her chair and rose. "I must check the pie."

Paul glanced at Susan and wilted. Making a visible effort to amend the situation, he said, "You should hear Estelle play piano. She used to play the pipe organ at our church in Madison, too."

"Might she be willing to play piano for our church?" Susan asked, turning to watch Estelle remove the berry pie from the oven. "Estelle, would you? We've had no pianist for years. The old piano just gathers dust."

"She could give music lessons, too," Margie suggested. "Flora has always wanted to play piano."

Flora nodded vigorously, her eyes glowing.

"If Miss Truman wishes to play piano for the church, we would all be grateful. We have plenty of hymnals." Frank watched her work at the counter, keeping her back to the table. "Not that I wish to impose, Miss Truman."

"I shall be pleased to play the pianoforte for Sunday meetings." She laid down a knife and squared her shoulders. "This pie needs to cool for a time before I slice it."

"Let's go sit on the porch and enjoy the evening," Susan suggested.

Dishes clinked and flatware clanked in the tin dishpans as Margie and Estelle hurried to use the last minutes of twilight. Two cats plumped on the kitchen windowsill, tails curled around their tucked feet, yellow eyes intent on the aerial dance of fireflies and bats above the lawn. Stars already twinkled in the pink and purple sky over the small orchard of fruit trees.

Although barnyard odors occasionally offended Estelle's nose, she savored the stillness of a country evening. Perhaps Iowa was a small corner of heaven, for her new life here held an almost magical charm. She found the big boys, Joshua and Alvin, somewhat boisterous and intimidating, though they spoke to her kindly and complimented her cooking. Gangly young Joe seemed aloof, but she suspected he was merely shy. Marjorie treated her like a bosom friend, and little Flora hung on her every word. Susan seemed grateful for her assistance with the housework.

Paul was the only fly in her ointment. *Aunt Bridget, indeed!*

"Tell me what you think of David, Auntie Stell," Margie said, rousing Estelle from her reverie. "Don't you think he's handsome?"

She contrived an honest compliment. "He has kind eyes."

"Doesn't he? Bluer than blue, with those thick yellow lashes. And I love his golden hair and his dimples. He sunburns easily, but in the winter his skin gets white like marble. I call him my Viking."

"I had the same thought." David's parson father required only a Wagnerian opera score to accompany his clumsy swagger.

"Did you?" Margie gave a delighted chuckle. "The pastor looks even more like a Viking with his bushy beard. I was afraid of him when I was little because he's so big and has such a loud laugh, but I soon figured out how kind he was."

Recalling the pastor's sympathetic expression and obvious efforts to please, Estelle felt a twinge of guilt. There was more to the man than enormous feet and a forceful voice. His sermon that morning had been excellent.

Susan entered, carrying a lamp. "Why are you two working in the dark?"

"Our eyes had adjusted," Margie said. "It didn't seem dark until you brought in the lamp. But now I can see better to wipe off the table. We're almost finished, Mama. David had to leave, so I plan to spend the evening sewing."

"The rest of the family is in the parlor, absorbed in newspapers and checkers. Pastor Nelson said to tell you both good-bye, and he'll see you in the morning, Estelle."

"Isn't he nice, Auntie? I'm so glad you'll be helping him with his book. David says he had about given up on ever finishing it, so you're an answer to prayer. You should see the pastor's study—papers everywhere!"

"It will also be wonderful to have a pianist for our church," Susan said as she placed glasses in a cupboard. "We haven't had one since Kirsten Nelson passed away."

"Reverend Nelson's wife played the piano?" Estelle asked.

"The church piano was hers," Susan said. "You can set those plates back on the china dresser if you like, Estelle. I can never thank you enough for your work around the house. You're a godsend to all of us, and no mistake." She gave Estelle's shoulders a quick squeeze and returned to her task. "I can't recall the last time I felt so rested of an evening."

Estelle couldn't recall the last time anyone had thanked her, let alone hugged her.

"Mrs. Nelson was a nice lady," Margie continued, "cheery and friendly. I remember how she always played hymns so high that no one could sing them. And we sang the same five songs over and over. David says they were the only hymns she knew."

"Marjorie, that is unkind."

"I don't mean it to be unkind. I liked Mrs. Nelson. I sometimes wonder if Pastor should move in with David and me after we marry, to be certain he eats meals and gets his wash done. David says Mary Bilge causes more dirt and mess than she cleans up. She'd probably go back to drinking if Pastor fired her, so he keeps her on."

Estelle hung her apron on a hook and straightened

her hair. "If you don't mind, I'll do some sewing tonight as well."

"Of course I don't mind! I want you to teach me how to make piping and those tiny ruffles." Margie caught her aunt by the hand and towed her upstairs.

Chapter 3

F rank shifted a stack of papers from one chair to another, then placed a second stack on top. No, that last pile needed to be separate. He moved it to the first chair and used a rock as a paperweight. When he slid a stack of books aside to search, it tipped. He grabbed at the sliding top book, but it eluded his grasp and landed open on his boot. Then the bottom half of the stack disintegrated and dropped to the floor with successive plops. He juggled two last books, caught one by its flyleaf, and watched the page rip out.

A morning breeze wafted the tattered window curtains, and notes fluttered about the room like moths. A horse whinnied outside. Hoofbeats passed the house. Frank ducked to peer outside. Estelle Truman, regal upon the seat of a dogcart, drove toward the barn.

Frank dropped the flyleaf and abandoned his study. Hearing the screen door slam, Miss Truman stopped her horse and looked over her shoulder. "Good morning, Reverend Nelson."

He took the veranda steps in two strides. "Good morning. I'll unhitch your horse today. Since you'll be coming regularly, I'll hire a boy to care for him from now on."

"You are kind." A hint of surprise colored her voice as she accepted his assistance to climb down. "Paul says Pepper can be difficult to catch. It might be best to stable him." She reached back to lift a covered basket from the cart.

"On such a fine day, I'll put him in the paddock with Bessie. Don't worry. If he gives us trouble later, we'll bribe him with carrots." Frank grinned, wondering if anything could make her smile.

"If you say so. Shall I begin work in your study?"

"Uh, you might want to wait for me. How about. . . how about you make tea again?"

She lifted one brow. "Most men prefer coffee."

"I like both," he said, stroking Pepper's forehead. The pony began to rub its face against his belly. Miss Truman's eyes followed the motion and widened. She tucked her chin, turned, and walked away, her swishing skirts raising a cloud of dust.

Once his new secretary had entered the house, Frank looked down at his blue plaid shirt and found it coated with horse saliva and white hair. "Thank you, Pepper," he muttered.

Freed of his harness, the pony bucked about the paddock, sniffed noses with the swaybacked mare, then collapsed to roll in the dust. Frank stowed the dogcart in his barn, hung up the harness, and rushed toward the house. Miss Truman must not see his study until he had a chance to pick up that last avalanche.

He stopped inside the kitchen door. The tea tray waited on the kitchen table. A basket of blackberry muffins and a bowl of canned peaches sat beside his filled teacup. Miss Truman poured hot water from the kettle into the dishpan, whipping up suds with her hand. The black cat rubbed against her skirts, purring.

"I brought muffins from home. Flora thought you might enjoy them. I found the peaches in your cellar. While you drink your tea, I'll wash up these dishes. Is Miss Bilge off duty today?"

"She usually shows up late. You don't have to do that." He waved at the dishpan.

"I cannot concentrate in an untidy environment. Tomorrow I shall come earlier to prepare your tea. The morning is already half gone. At the office in Madison,

I began work at seven each day."

"And how late did you work?" Frank sat at the table, bowed his head to give silent but fervent thanks, and picked up a muffin.

"Until seven at night. I shall be unable to work that late here, however, for I must help with chores at home." She scrubbed dishes as she spoke. "My mother became accustomed to dining late."

"You prepared supper for your mother after working twelve-hour days?" He polished off his second muffin and took a sip of tea.

"When Aunt Bridget was alive, she cooked. After her death. . ." Her shoulders lifted and fell. "We lived simply." She wiped down the countertops, the stovetop, and the worktable. Sinews appeared in her forearms as she wrung out the dishcloth. Hefting the dishpan, she carried it outside. He heard water splash into the garden.

Only then did she take another cup and saucer from the cupboard and pour herself a cup of tea. "May I carry this into the study?"

He nodded and stood up. "I'll carry the tray." He didn't want to leave those muffins behind. But then, picturing the study as he had last seen it, he realized there would be no place to set a teacup, let alone a tray. "Wait."

When she gave him an inquisitive look, her eyes were almost pretty.

"Let me go in first and pick up. I. . .had trouble this morning."

"You hired me to make order from chaos, Reverend Nelson. Please direct me to the study and trust me to earn my pay, which, by the way, has not yet been discussed."

"Down the hall and to the right." To the left of the hall lay the parlor, which completed the house's main floor plan. Upstairs were two small bedrooms, and below the kitchen lurked the earth-walled cellar, where she had found the peaches. Not much in this tiny parsonage to interest a cultured woman.

Estelle took a sip of her tea and set the cup and saucer on the table. With a lift of her chin, she swept past him into the hall, her skirts brushing his legs. Belle trotted after her, trilling a feline love song. The study door creaked open. Frank sat down, crossed his forearms on the table, and dropped his head to rest upon them. A silent plea moved his lips.

The screen door slammed, and his heart gave a jolt. Tea sloshed on the table from the two cups, and a muffin fell from the basket. Halfway to his feet, he gaped at Mary Bilge.

"You sick, Preacher?" Her dark eyes scanned the tidy

kitchen, the teapot, and the muffins—and narrowed. "Eating sweets at this hour musta soured your stomach. What you need is strong coffee." She filled the coffeepot from the pump, poured in a quantity of grounds from the canister, and clanged the pot on the stovetop. "Reckon I'll put on beans to soak for supper before I start the laundry."

Frank nodded. Beans again. He took another muffin. "No coffee, thanks. I've got calls to make."

"She gonna be here all day?" Mary jerked her head toward the study. Beans rattled into a cast-iron pot. She dropped the empty gunnysack, placed the pot in the sink, and pumped until water gushed to cover the beans.

"Yes. Let me lift that, Mary. You want it on the stovetop?" Frank couldn't sit by and watch a woman heft such a load.

"Yup." Mary grinned at him. "I'll keep an eye out to make sure that woman don't cheat you."

Frank hoisted the pot to the stove. "Want this over the heat?"

"No, it's just gotta soak a few hours. You go on, Preacher. I ain't no city lady with skinny arms and a frozen heart. You can rely on me. I'll do your wash today."

Frank smoothed his hair as he approached the study. Still in the hall, he heard Estelle give a little cough, then the shuffle of papers. "Miss Truman, I have calls to make. I'll be back after midday. Can you cope alone until then?" He closed his eyes while waiting for her answer, feeling like a coward.

"Yes, Reverend Nelson. Remember to wear a clean shirt."

He glanced down at himself and brushed at the imbedded hair. "Of course." *If I can find one.*

Minutes later, he cantered Powder through the stable yard and out the gate. August sun baked his shoulders and wind whipped his cheeks, but for a few blessed hours he was free from controlling women.

First he visited the Dixons and their recovering baby. He prayed over the tiny boy, rejoiced in his increasing strength, and promised to return soon. Althea Dixon gave him a hug and a jar of tomatoes before he left. She reminded him of his own daughter, Amy.

While riding to his next call, he wondered about Estelle. Upon his return, would she resign her position and inform him that his scribblings could never form a book? Would her cool blue eyes mock his pretensions? A confusing blend of fears troubled his heart.

In a sunlit sitting room at the rambling Coon homestead, old Beatrice Coon talked with him at length about family concerns, particularly one great-grandson. "Jubal's boy, Abel, is shiftless and sly. I pray for him every day, as I do for all my loved ones, but I do believe the boy is deaf to the Lord's call. His great-grandfather surely turned in his grave when Abel left college." She dabbed tears from her wrinkled cheeks.

Frank sympathized, well aware that Abel had been expelled from the university. The young man was rapidly becoming a bane to the community as well as a sorrow to the honorable Coon family.

When Frank made noises about heading out, Beatrice protested. "Why so restless today, Pastor Frank? You can't be leaving without reading to me from the Good Book."

Although Mrs. Coon lived with her grandson Sheldon's large and literate family, any member of which could have read to her throughout the day, Frank couldn't deny her request. She rocked in her chair and knitted while he read, and when he did finally say good-bye, she handed him a blue stocking cap with a tassel. "Soon the snows will be upon us, and you'll find it useful to warm places your pretty yellow hair doesn't cover anymore."

His hand lifted to the thinning patch on top of his head, and he returned her grin. "Thanks, Mrs. Coon."

"I made it to match your eyes," she said with a feminine titter. "Can you blame an old woman for keeping a handsome man near using any means she has?"

Freedom from controlling women was a pipe dream. He chuckled, squeezed her gnarled hands, and prayed with her before he left. Being near the feisty octogenarian made him feel young and spry, a rare sensation since the passing of his fiftieth birthday last spring.

As he entered town and approached the parsonage, he noticed the rundown condition of Mary Bilge's house across the way. Mary's personal habits seemed unaffected by her profession of faith. True, she no longer inhabited the saloons, a mark in her favor. But her slovenly attire, cigar smoking, and lack of ambition persisted. Hiring her as housekeeper had been his daughter Amy's idea, a kind-hearted attempt to build up Mary's dignity. Instead of dignity, Mary seemed to have developed expectations Frank would rather not think about.

Pepper whinnied a greeting from the paddock. Young Harmon Coon, another of Beatrice's great-grandsons, should arrive soon to hitch up the old pony. Frank trusted the boy to keep his end of the bargain. Those Coons were principled people. A founding family to be proud of, despite their one black sheep.

Frank's laundry waved from the line behind the house, neatly pinned. Shirts, trousers, combinations, nightshirt, all looked. . .clean. Kitchen towels and dishcloths gleamed white under the summer sun.

As he mounted the veranda steps, a pleasant aroma made him stop and sniff. Had Mary baked bread? Maybe the perceived competition from Miss Truman had prodded her into action. Brows lifted, Frank pursed his lips in a soundless whistle and let the screen door slam shut.

He placed the jar of tomatoes on the kitchen counter. "Hello?" Belle, curled on a kitchen chair, lifted her head to blink at him sleepily. Two towel-draped mounds on the countertop drew his attention. He peeked under the towel and nearly drooled at the sight and smell of warm, crusty loaves. Something bubbled on the stove. He lifted the lid of a saucepan to find not beans but a simmering vegetable soup.

Mary Bilge could not create such artistry if her life depended on it. Had she and Estelle fought for control of the house? How would two women fight? Flat irons at ten paces? Rolling pins to the death? The mental image of Belle the cat battling a mangy upstart to maintain her queenly status made him smile. No wonder the cat had bonded with her human counterpart. However—his smile faded—Mary had been here first.

The only way to find out for certain what had occurred was to ask. "Miss Truman?" He pushed open the study door and actually saw carpeting instead of books and papers. His gaze lifted to discover shelves full of books, papers stacked on the desk, and his flighty notes weighted by the rock. The file cabinet stood open, and Miss Truman appeared to be labeling files.

She had removed her jacket. A tailored shirtwaist emphasized her slim figure. No longer did she look scrawny to Frank. He knew her as a creative powerhouse. How had the woman accomplished so much in one day? And she still managed to look unruffled.

She glanced up. "Reverend Nelson, I require your assistance. I believe it would be helpful to create an individual file for each topic or chapter of your book. As I look over your outline, I see distinct categories which will simplify this task."

His heart thundered in his ears. "You do?"

"Yes. We should also file your published periodical articles along with their research material in case you decide to reuse any of them in your books. My suggestion would be to create a file for each doctrinal issue—eschatology, predestination, divine attributes, and so forth. You may discover a need for further breakdown of these categories, but this will give us a start."

"A start," he echoed. While she continued to describe her system, he moved closer and looked over her shoulder at the miraculous way his stacks of paper fit neatly into her files. She smelled of fresh bread and soap. Although her skin betrayed her advancing age, sagging slightly beneath her pointed chin and crinkling around her eyes and mouth, it looked soft to touch. She must be near fifty, since she was Paul's elder sister. Just the right age.

Her eyes were like diamonds with blue edges, keen and cool, focused on his face. He suddenly realized that she had asked him a question. "Pardon?"

"I asked if you were planning to work on your manuscript tonight. If you prepare a few pages, I'll transcribe them for you tomorrow. I do request that you attempt to write more clearly. Some of your letters are illegible."

"Can you. . .can you write from dictation?"

"Yes, although I find that few people organize their thoughts well enough to dictate good literature." She tucked one last sheaf of paper into the file, slid the drawer shut, and leaned her back against it. Her expression as she surveyed the room revealed gratification. "A promising beginning to our work, Reverend. Tomorrow I shall clean this room before we begin."

The thought of her returning in the morning warmed him clear through. "I noticed the bread and soup in the kitchen. Mary had planned beans for tonight. I don't see her around anywhere. What happened?"

Her long fingers rubbed the corner of the file cabinet, and her gaze lowered. Pink tinged her cheekbones.

"I smelled the beans burning and went to stir them. Reverend, she did not rinse the beans, and they had not soaked long enough to soften before she set them to boil. You would have had crunchy beans for supper tonight, along with rocks and sticks."

It wouldn't have been the first time. "And the laundry?"

Her lips tightened into a straight line. "She was washing your clothes without soap and draping them over the line dripping wet."

"So what did you do?"

"I advised her to use soap. She dropped your. . .uh, garment in the dirt, called me some unrepeatable names, and walked away. I have not seen her since."

"So you washed my laundry, baked bread, cooked my dinner, and filed my papers, all while I was away for a few hours. Miss Truman, you will exhaust yourself at this pace."

Her gaze snapped back to his. "Nonsense. I enjoyed myself." Suddenly her color deepened. With a quick lift of her chin, she slipped around him and headed for the entryway. "I had better leave, since my chaperone is missing."

He followed her. "You won't stay for soup?"

Tying her bonnet strings, she glanced up at him then away. "They will expect me at home. The soup should be ready for you to eat. I made it with canned vegetables from your cellar and a bit of bacon."

She opened the front door. Pepper, harnessed to the dogcart, waited at the hitching rail out front. Afternoon light dotted the lawn beneath the trees, and sunflowers bobbed in a breeze. "Good day, Reverend Nelson. I shall return in the morning."

"You'll make tea?" He wanted her to look at him.

"Yes, but you need to purchase more." When she gazed into the distance, her eyes reflected the sky. "You need to bring in your laundry. It should be dry."

"I'll do that. Thank you, Miss Truman."

"It was my pleasure. I'll iron tomorrow." She hurried down the walkway and climbed into the cart. Frank watched her drive away. Almost as soon as she disappeared from view, he set out down the street toward the general store to stock up on tea.

Later, after piling his clean laundry into a basket, he sliced bread and buttered it, then ladled out soup into a truly clean bowl. He spooned a bite into his mouth. Slightly spicy, rich, and hot. Perfect with the tender bread. He ate his fill, then put the rest away for lunch tomorrow. Remembering Estelle at his sink, sleeves rolled up as she scrubbed, he rinsed his supper dishes and stacked them in the dishpan. In a happy daze, he sat and rocked on his veranda until evening shadows fell.

How could this be? A man his age couldn't be fool enough to fall in love with a woman for her cooking. He scarcely knew Estelle Truman, yet his heart sang like a mockingbird every time she entered his thoughts.

"Lord, what do I do now? I don't even know if she's a believer, though she spoke about doctrine with familiarity. She is so serious and. . .and cold." His brows lowered as he remembered Paul's analogy.

Although his memories were fading, he still recalled Kirsten's round, rosy face with its almost perpetual smile. Plump, blond, and talkative, she had been Estelle's exact opposite. No, not exact. Kirsten had been a good cook and housekeeper, too.

"And she loved me," he murmured. "I wonder if Estelle could love me."

Warmth brushed his leg, and a cat hopped into his lap. Belle, of course, purring and almost maudlin in her demand for affection. He rubbed her cheeks and chin, assured her of her surpassing beauty, and stroked her silken body while she nuzzled his beard and trilled. Of course, if he had picked her up uninvited, she would have cut him dead with one glance, growled, and struggled to be free.

"Is Estelle like my cat, Lord? Maybe she'll respond to undemanding affection. How does a man go about courting a woman who's forgotten how to love?" He sighed. "Why do I have the feeling I'm going to get scratched if I try?"

Chapter 4

Cold seeped through the study windows as a late October wind moaned around the parsonage. Frank lifted the new calico curtain to reveal a gray early morning, then settled back in his desk chair with a contented smile. Soon Estelle would come and turn the cold, empty house into a home.

Since she had arrived in August, his life had exchanged confusion for comfort. Organization had never assumed a more appealing form. Even Mary now accomplished work around the house—sweeping, dusting, beating rugs, and laundering. Frank suspected the woman hadn't known how to keep house until Estelle trained her.

And music had returned to the church. From his seat on the platform, Frank could watch Estelle's profile as she played piano for the morning service each week. Since her arrival, people had started requesting a longer song service, Lionel Coon had led the singing with renewed enthusiasm, and attendance had increased until there would soon be need for two Sunday services unless the church could afford to enlarge the sanctuary. Whatever the board decided was fine with Frank. More people heard God's Word each week—that was the important thing.

He occasionally finagled a supper invitation out of Paul and had opportunity to observe Estelle in her brother's household. Frank sought evidence of thawing around her heart, but she seemed as detached and cool as ever. Flora obviously adored her maiden aunt. Did Estelle care at all for the child? Margie raved about her aunt's needlework; Estelle had helped design the wedding gown and the gowns for the attendants. Yet did she derive any pleasure from her accomplishments? Thanks to Estelle's help around the house, Susan had regained much of her strength. Although Susan rained affection and appreciation upon her, Estelle appeared to endure rather than enjoy her sister-in-law's attention.

Only once had Frank witnessed affection from Estelle Truman. Its recipient had been, of all things, Belle the cat. Returning early from a call, he had stopped at the post office, then entered his house quietly, examining his mail. Hearing talk in the study, he had approached and stopped outside the door, amazed to recognize the cooing voice as Estelle's. Loud purring plus an occasional trilling meow identified her companion. Another step revealed the tableau to his astonished gaze. Estelle cradled the fawning creature in her arms and rubbed her face against Belle's glossy fur, wearing a tender expression that stole Frank's breath away.

The floor had creaked, revealing his presence. Two startled faces had looked up at him. Belle leaped to the floor and scooted past his feet. Estelle brushed cat hair from her gown and turned away, but not before he witnessed her deep blush. He could not recall what had been said in those awkward moments.

Would Estelle ever look at him with warmth in her eyes? After all these weeks, he still felt uncertain in her presence. While she no longer openly scorned him, neither did he receive affectionate glances from her. They frequently shared pleasant companionship, sipping tea while discussing the arrangement of paragraphs or catching up on community news. She pampered him with delicious meals and fresh-baked bread. Yet she maintained an emotional distance that discouraged thoughts of romance.

He entertained such thoughts anyway. Kirsten had often accused him of being a hopeless romantic; perhaps it was true. A more hopeless romance than this he could scarcely imagine.

Returning to the present, he flipped through notes for the final chapter of his book. The last chapter. How had it all happened so quickly? Estelle insisted the book had been complete before her arrival; she had simply put his notes in coherent order. He knew better. The book never would have been written without her. How had he survived before she entered his life? He never wanted to return to the colorless, disordered existence he had endured since Kirsten's death.

If he could convince Estelle to marry him, his problems would be over. Well, some of his problems. Actually, marriage often presented a new set of problems. Despite his prayers for God's leading, he hesitated when it came to proposing. Maybe God had been trying to show him that such a union would never work. Or maybe he feared rejection. Estelle might fix her keen gaze on him and question his sanity. His touch might fill her with loathing. With a groan, he crossed his arms and laid his head on his desk.

Oh, to be a cat.

"Reverend Nelson?" He lifted his head and turned, blinking at the embodiment of his dream. "I saw the lamplight. Did you spend the night here?" Estelle's gaze flickered across his manuscript.

He rubbed his stiff neck and rolled his head and shoulders. "No, I rose early to work. I never heard you drive up."

"It's windy today. Paul says a storm may be coming." When she approached to open the curtains and let in morning light, her full skirts brushed his left arm. "It's cold in here. I built up the fire in the stove. You'd better come into the kitchen until the house warms up. I'll make pancakes if you like, or oatmeal."

"Pancakes, please. And tea, as long as you drink it with me." He followed her to the kitchen. Belle greeted him, winding around his feet. He pulled a chair near the stove, let Belle hop into his lap, and watched Estelle work. Her every movement seemed to him graceful and efficient. Like poetry or music.

While whipping eggs for pancake batter, Estelle glanced at him. "You're quiet this morning. Did you accomplish much work?"

"No. I was thinking about you."

For an instant, her spoon froze in place; then slowly, she began to stir again. After greasing the griddle, she poured four small circles of batter. "Since the book is nearly complete, I imagine my employment here will soon end."

"I don't know what I'd do without you."

She swallowed hard. Once she opened her mouth to speak, then closed it. "I don't understand."

He wanted to stand up, turn her to face him, and declare his love—but he knew better. Like Belle, she would struggle and growl and resent his advances.

"You have become part of my life. Part of me. I can't imagine a future without you here in my home every day." He rubbed the back of his neck again. "If I have your consent, I want to ask your brother for permission to court you."

She looked like a marble statue: *Woman with Spatula.*

"The pancakes are burning."

Breath burst from her, and she flipped the cakes. "But why?"

He almost made a quip about things burning when they cook too long but thought better of it. "I think you're a wonderful woman, Estelle."

She sucked in a breath and closed her eyes.

Encouraged, he elaborated. "You are accomplished and creative and thoughtful. Out of the kindness of your heart, you have made my house back into a home, so much so that I hate to leave whenever you're here. You've trained Mary Bilge into a decent housekeeper, a miracle in itself. Your list of piano students lengthens daily. Without a word of complaint, you took a disastrous mass of scribbling and turned it into an organized manuscript, possibly worthy of publication."

She snapped back into motion, rescued the pancakes, and poured a new batch, scraping out the bowl. Quickly she buttered the cakes and sprinkled them with brown sugar. "Eat them while they're hot."

"Thank you." He bowed his head, adding a plea for wisdom.

When he opened his eyes and began to eat, she was staring at the griddle. "You don't really know me."

He finished chewing a bite and swallowed. "I want to know you better. Everything I see, I like. Is there hope for me, Estelle?"

She turned the pancakes. "I need time to think."

"Do you want to take the rest of today off?"

After a pause, she nodded. "I'll clean the kitchen first."

"When you're ready, I'll hitch Pepper."

Frank attempted to work on his manuscript, but concentration was impossible. He needed to be with Estelle, needed to know her thoughts. At last he gave up, saddled Powder, and rode to the Trumans' farm. Susan greeted him at the door, and Paul came from the barn. "What brings you out this blustery day, Frank?" he asked, wiping axle grease from his hands with a rag.

"Come inside out of the cold," Susan said.

Frank stepped into the entry. "I'm looking for Estelle."

Susan closed the door behind Paul and took Frank's hat and scarf. "She came home for a short time and left again. I thought she must have forgotten something; she never said a word."

"Did she take anything with her?" Fear shortened Frank's breath.

"I'll go look," Susan offered, then hurried upstairs.

"You might as well tell us what happened. I can guess, but it's easier to ask." Paul led him toward the kitchen, where Eliza left her warm bed by the stove and came wagging to greet him.

After patting the dog, Frank slumped into a kitchen chair and accepted a cup of coffee. "This morning I told her I planned to ask your permission to court her. She said she needed time to think, so I gave her the rest of the day off."

Paul set his own cup down and sat across from Frank. "You don't want to marry her, Frank. Trust me on this one."

Susan bustled in. "No, no, don't bother getting up; I'll join you in a moment. Estelle's trunk is open, and it looks as if she took something from inside, but her clothing and bags are all here. What happened, Frank? Did you propose to her? I know you're in love with her. I think everyone in town knows."

Heat flowed up his neck in a wave.

"Estelle is a good enough person, I guess," Paul said, "but she would make a poor choice of wife. She closed her heart to love twenty years ago."

"What happened then?" Frank asked.

Paul sipped his coffee and grimaced. "She was engaged to a ministerial student by the name of John Forster. A sober fellow with social aspirations. When the war started, he joined up as chaplain. Made it through the war unscathed, then died of a fever before he could return home. Estelle was furious with God."

Frank bowed his head. "Understandable."

"Yes, but she never got over it. She turned bitter and heartless. When I brought my wife home to meet the family, my only sister rejected her simply because she had worked as a maid."

Susan shook her head. "Now that's not entirely true, Paul. Estelle stood with her parents in public, but before we left, she secretly gave me that heirloom pin of your grandmother's. I think she felt bad about the way your parents behaved, but who could stand up against your father? He terrified me. I can't blame her for bowing to his will."

Paul huffed. "You're too forgiving."

"Can anyone be too forgiving?" Frank asked, turning his cup between his hands.

"Paul, tell about when you wrote to your parents," Susan said.

He sighed deeply. "Around two years ago, you preached a series of sermons on forgiveness, Frank. I wrote to my parents, trying to restore the relationship. Estelle wrote back to tell me that our father had died soon after Susan and I moved away, leaving them penniless. Estelle had been working at a law office all those years to support our mother and, for a time, our great-aunt. Mother never answered my letter."

"And you didn't contact Estelle again until she wrote to inform you of your mother's death," Susan said.

"Which was when Paul came to me," Frank finished the tale, "and asked if I would hire her as secretary. She's had a lonely, disappointing life from the sound of it."

"True, but she didn't have to freeze into herself the way she did," Paul said. "Many people endure heartbreak and disappointment without becoming icebergs. As a child, Estelle was lively, full of mischief, loving toward me. She wept when I went off to war, and she wrote to me faithfully. I told her about my new wife in my letters, and she seemed excited. And then to have her reject us so coldly. . ."

Paul shook his head. "She's worse now than ever."

"I think she is afraid to love," Susan said.

"I think she's angry at God," Paul insisted.

"I think I need to find out the truth from her," Frank decided. "Thanks for the coffee. I'll hunt for her around town. I have an idea where she is."

Chapter 5

Frank let Powder gallop toward the church. Gray clouds scudded across the vast sky. With the fields harvested, a man could see for miles. A raucous flock of crows passed overhead and faded into the distance. Wind tugged at Frank's hat, trying to rip it from his head.

The church's white steeple beckoned as if promising refuge. As Frank expected, Pepper dozed in the shed out back, still hitched to the dogcart. When the wind shifted, tempestuous music filled the air.

Frank opened the church doors and slipped inside. The music increased in volume again when he opened the sanctuary door. Estelle sat at the piano, her sheet music lit by tapers in the instrument's folding candle racks. Her strong hands flew over the keys. Frank thought he recognized Beethoven, a violent piece. Its intensity covered his footsteps until he could slide into a seat four rows behind her. When the song ended, she turned a few pages and played a yearning sonata, then moved on to several complex and stirring works of art. After a pause, she performed a hauntingly romantic piece. The music flowing from her fingers brought tears to Frank's eyes.

As the last notes faded away, she clenched her fists beneath her chin and hunched over.

"I've never heard anything more beautiful," Frank said.

Estelle hit the keyboard with both palms as if to catch herself. Instantly she jerked her hands up to end the discordant jangle and glanced at Frank over her shoulder. "I didn't hear you enter." She checked the watch pinned to her shirtwaist, exclaimed softly, closed her book, and slid the felt keyboard cover into place. "How long have you been here?"

Frank rose and approached the piano. "Not long enough. Whatever you were playing there was powerful. Music for the soul."

Estelle avoided his gaze. "Thank you."

"I felt, while listening, that at last I was seeing and hearing the real Estelle."

"Your wife played. Does it bother you to hear me play her piano?"

He rubbed one hand across the piano's top, then

brushed dust from his fingers. "Kirsten never played like you do. Her music was cheery and uncomplicated, a reflection of her personality. Your music is rich and passionate, a reflection of your soul."

With shaking hands, Estelle began to gather up her music. "That was Schubert, not me."

He lowered his voice. "Paul and Susan told me about John Forster's untimely death. Paul believes you're angry with God. Susan believes you're afraid to love. I wonder if both are correct."

She paused. "If they are, my feelings are justified."

"Tell me."

Her oblique gaze pierced him. "Why should I?"

"As I said this morning, I want to know you. And I think you need to talk. Anything you say is confidential; I will tell no one."

She breathed hard for a few moments, staring at the keyboard. "John didn't die in the war," she said with quiet intensity. "God took him from me. Then my parents rejected Susan, so Paul went away hating me. Then my father died of a heart attack, leaving behind debts that consumed his entire fortune. For twenty years, I slaved in an office to support my mother and my great-aunt, who spent the remainder of their lives complaining about my insufficient provision and warning me never to trust a man."

Frank could easily picture them, having encountered human leeches before. "Did your mother never work? I remember when Paul learned of your financial ruin—long after the event, I'm sorry to say. He told me how socially ambitious and dependent your mother was and wondered how you managed her."

"Mother took to her bed years ago, though she was not truly ill until last winter. Doubtless you will think me a monster, but I have shed no tears since her passing. Her death came as a blessed release, as did Aunt Bridget's demise ten years earlier. The last person I mourned was my father, the model husband and father, who betrayed us all by keeping a second family on the far side of town. The other woman made her claim after his death."

Frank's jaw dropped.

"I did not want to believe her assertions, but once she proved my father's infidelity, I did right by my five half brothers and sisters. They are all grown men and women by now; at the time, they were helpless children."

"Does Paul know any of this?"

"No. When it occurred, I was unaware of his location. He contacted us a few years ago. Mother refused to acknowledge him, so I wrote to him secretly."

"He told me what happened when he brought Susan home with him after the war."

"She had been a housemaid. Far too good for any of us Trumans, actually." Estelle closed her eyes. "At the time, I thought it my duty to uphold my parents' decision, but Paul will never forgive me. Oh, life is unpredictable and cruel!" Her voice broke.

"The people who should have loved and protected you failed you, Estelle." Frank spoke softly. "I understand your anger and your bitterness. I've had a share of heartbreak in my life, but unlike you, I've also had people who loved me faithfully."

"The only people who might have loved me, God took away."

"That's not entirely true."

She glared at him. "Now I'm to hear the sermon about God's faithful love."

Frowning to conceal his hurt, he rubbed his beard. "I didn't know I annoyed you so much."

He heard her sigh. "I apologize. That accusation was unkind and unfair. Your Sunday sermons challenge my mind, as does your book, yet often when you preach, I hear only riddles and contradictions. 'God's plan of salvation is simple,' you say, yet as I work on your manuscript, I am overwhelmed by the complexity of the Christian creed."

"I thought you understood."

Shaking her head, she watched her fingers fold pleats

in her skirt. "Aunt Bridget told me that my salvation lay in religion and duty. I have done my best, but sometimes the loneliness is too much to bear."

"Good works cannot regenerate your sinful spirit or mine. Our righteousness is as filthy rags in God's sight. He must transform us from the inside out."

"But what if He doesn't?" The pain in Estelle's expression tore at his heart. "I do believe that Jesus is God's Son, sent to earth to die in my place, but my belief seems to make no difference. What if I'm not one of His chosen ones?"

Frank prayed for the right words. "Belief involves more than an intellectual acceptance of fact. It involves acknowledgment of your unworthy condition, surrender of the will, dying to self. If you come to Him, He will certainly not cast you out."

Emotions flickered across her face—longing, defiance, resolve. "You say God is love and God is all-powerful. If He is both, how can there be sin, deceit, murder, and ugliness in this world? Why do innocent people suffer? Why doesn't God allow everyone into heaven if He loves us all so much?"

"We're all sinners. One evidence of God's love is that He doesn't simply give us what we deserve—eternal damnation. Instead, He offers everyone the opportunity to love and serve Him or to reject His gift of salvation."

She nodded slowly.

Encouraged, he continued, "Each day of your life you choose between good and evil, as do the murderers and liars and adulterers of this world. Our choices affect the people around us, and the more those people love us, the more deeply they are affected. You have chosen a life of isolation rather than to risk the vulnerability that comes with love." As soon as the words left his lips, he knew he'd made a mistake.

Shaking visibly, she leaped to her feet and poked her forefinger into his chest. "You have no right to judge me!"

He bowed his head. "It's true. I have no right to judge; only God has that right. For a man who makes his living with words, I'm bad at expressing my feelings. Because I care, I want you to share the abundant life God gives, but the choice is yours to make."

She folded her arms across her chest and stared at the floor. "You ask me to risk everything by loving a God who has never yet shown Himself worthy of my faith."

"The request for your faith comes from God, not from me. He said a Savior would come to earth, and He did; we celebrate that kept promise at Christmas. He said He would die for us, and He did; we commemorate that sacrifice on Good Friday. He said He would conquer death and rise again, and He did; we rejoice in that triumphant victory at Easter. You can trust Him to keep His promises, Estelle. He desires your love and trust enough to die for you."

Estelle's head jerked back. "I need to go home."

Frank swallowed hasty words and bowed his head. "Yes, it grows late. I'll follow you home."

Outside, the wind knifed them with the chill of winter. Estelle clutched her shawl around herself and gasped. Frank closed the church doors. "You need more than a shawl in this wind. We can stop at the parsonage for blankets and coats. I think we might get snow overnight."

He took Estelle's hand and led her back to the shed where the horses waited. Without protest, she let him tie Powder up behind the dogcart, climb in beside her, and drive through the dark churchyard to the main road. Wind whipped trees and scattered leaves across the road.

"Hang on to me, if you want," he offered, raising his voice above the wind. She immediately gripped his arm and buried her face against his shoulder. He grinned into the gale.

When Pepper stopped in front of the parsonage, Frank heard Estelle's teeth chattering. "Come in for hot tea before I take you home." He rubbed her unresisting fingers. "Your hands are like ice."

"But it's nearly dark," she protested.

"Just for a moment." He helped her from the cart. Within minutes, he was stoking the fire in the oven and filling the kettle. Seeing Estelle shiver, he hurried to find blankets.

When he returned, she was pouring tea. Lamplight turned her eyes to fire as she glanced up. "I hope Susan doesn't worry."

"I told her I would find you. She won't worry." He accepted his teacup and pulled two chairs close to the stove. "Wrap this blanket around your shoulders and soak up that warmth. We can't stay long, you're right, but I want to feel heat in your hands before we head home."

She nodded and obeyed, huddled beside him beneath a quilt. "I shall consider what we discussed at the church," she said. "I plan to read the Bible while looking for the principles you laid out in your book. Until tonight I thought them mere dogma, intellectual pursuits, and I privately mocked your insistence upon applying scripture to everyday life."

He sipped his tea to conceal his reaction to the affront.

"I shall pray for insight as I read." She laid her hand on his arm and peered up into his face. "Reverend Nelson, I must thank you for taking time to hear my tale and offer your sage advice. I understand why your parishioners seek your counsel. You are a man of many gifts that were not immediately evident to me."

He swallowed the last of his tea and stood up. "We must be off. Wrap up in that quilt, and I'll bring another for your feet." She had met and exceeded his one criterion—warm hands. The imprint of her hand would burn on his arm for hours to come.

"Thanks for bringing Estelle home, Frank," Paul said while Susan poured hot coffee. The four sat near the glowing oven in Susan's kitchen. "You can sleep on the sofa tonight. I already told Josh to stable your horse. It's no night to be on the road."

"I appreciate the shelter." Frank studied Estelle in concern while speaking to Paul. "That wind held an awful bite. Wouldn't be surprised to see snow on the ground come morning." Would she take ill from exposure? He had tried to protect her from the wind, but she still looked pale.

Paul frowned. "Estelle won't be returning to the parsonage. You can bring work here for her. From all I've heard, the book is nearly ready to submit to a publisher."

Estelle's head snapped around. "I most certainly will be working at the parsonage. I need access to the files. Why should Reverend Nelson have to bring my work here?"

"Because your situation has changed. Frank is court-ing you; therefore, it is no longer appropriate for you to work in his house. A minister must observe proprieties, perhaps even more carefully than most people do."

Frank barely concealed his surprise and dismay. He had interpreted Paul's earlier discouraging comments as a refusal of his courtship request. When had the story changed?

Estelle met Frank's gaze across the table. "But what will you eat?" As soon as the words left her lips, she flushed and looked away.

"Eat?" Paul said, glowering at Frank. "Is my sister a secretary or a cook? I don't like the sound of this."

"Now, Paul, I'm certain they have behaved properly," Susan inserted gently as she handed out steaming cups of coffee. "Don't jump to conclusions."

Embarrassment and frustration built in Frank's chest. "Thank you, Susan. You can rest assured that nothing untoward occurred while Miss Truman worked at the parsonage, but I respect Paul's decision. I don't mind bringing work here until the book is complete. I can drop by each morning before I make calls, and we can discuss progress and objectives then. I'll still pay her to complete the job."

Later that night, Frank wedged his frame into the confines of the hard horsehair sofa. Between the effect of strong coffee and the discomfort of a chilly parlor, he knew sleep would be long in coming, so he prayed. *Lord, I know now why I had no peace about proposing to Estelle. I was wrong to blurt out my feelings today, but at least we had our first meaningful discussion of You, and I know where she stands. I can't say I'm happy with the situation, but knowing is better than living in the dark.*

He rolled to his side, pulled a quilt over his shoulders, and felt a draft on his feet. *Much though I would like to, I can't blame my present dilemma on Paul. Today I, a minister of the gospel, declared my love to an unbeliever, and now we are officially courting. Calling myself all kinds of a fool also leaves the problem unsolved. What can I do? If I withdraw my offer of love, I'll be one more person letting her down. If I don't, she'll be expecting me to court her. . . .*

Chapter 6

Weeks passed, and Estelle's life again settled into a routine. Frank stopped by the Truman farm each day before beginning his round of calls or planning his sermons. He behaved like a pastor and friend; no hint of the ardent lover reappeared. Estelle began to wonder if he had changed his mind about courting her. Not that she intended to marry the man, of course. But as revisions on the book neared completion, she realized how much she would miss seeing Frank each day when he no longer had a reason to call.

Thanksgiving Day arrived. David joined the Truman family, but Frank traveled to Des Moines to visit his daughter, Amy, and her husband. Estelle helped prepare the Truman feast and took part in the family celebration, struggling to conceal her loneliness. When had Frank's presence become essential to her contentment? This need for him alarmed her. She needed to make a complete break if she was to maintain emotional independence.

One morning in mid-December, Frank dropped by as usual. Shaking snow from his overcoat, he let Estelle take his hat. "I brought out the cutter this morning. Winter is here to stay. Which reminds me, will you join me for the Christmas sleigh ride this year?"

Estelle hung his hat over his scarf. "Christmas sleigh ride?"

"You haven't heard about it? The sleigh ride is a Coon's Hollow tradition—when we have enough snow, that is. It's an unofficial event; people ride up and down the main streets and out into the countryside. Some of the young fellows have races, but us older folks prefer a decorous pace. My little cutter carries two in close comfort. I'll bundle you up with robes and hot bricks, and we'll put Powder through his paces." He looked into her eyes and smiled.

Despite the pastor's flushed face and disheveled hair, Estelle found him appealing. For the moment, her emotional independence diminished in value. "I shall be honored to join you."

His dimples deepened, and his eyes sparkled. He caught her hand and squeezed gently. "Soon we need to have another serious talk, Estelle." He glanced around, and Estelle became aware of Joe and Flora chatting in the kitchen. "Privacy is scarce these days."

Tightness built in Estelle's chest. Desperate to escape its demands, she pulled her hand from Frank's warm grasp and focused on the portfolio beneath his arm. "Did you make revisions on the final chapter?"

He blinked, and the sparkle faded. "I did. This next week I plan to read through the entire thing, and if no major flaws turn up, I'll mail it off to Chicago. My brother, who pastors a large church there, spoke with an editor who happens to attend his church. It seems this editor is eager to see the manuscript. I didn't seek these connections, but apparently God has been making them for me."

Hours later, Estelle lifted her pen and stared at the final page, revised as Frank had requested. After just over three months of work, the book was complete. She laid the paper atop her stack, selected a clean sheet, and dipped her pen again. The concluding chapter contained a scripture passage and application she wanted to keep for her own study. Reading Frank's words was the next best thing to hearing his sermons, and writing them down fixed them into her memory. Lately his explanations of

Bible passages seemed clearer, though she still often found herself perplexed.

Eliza, lying across Estelle's feet beneath the table, moaned in her sleep and twitched as if chasing a dream rabbit. Estelle rubbed the dog's white belly with the toe of her shoe.

She paused to flex her fingers and stare through the kitchen window. Where green lawn had once met her gaze, blindingly white snow now drifted in gentle waves. She imagined skimming over the snow in a cutter, snuggled close to Frank beneath warm robes, and a smile teased her lips. Often lately she sensed a hazy, tantalizing possibility, as if someone offered a future of beauty and hope but kept it always slightly out of her view.

Rapid footsteps entered the kitchen. "Would you care for a cup of tea, Auntie Stell?" Margie offered. "How is the book coming?"

"Thank you, yes," Estelle said. "My fingers need a rest. Have you finished sewing on the seed pearls?"

"Almost. They are perfect on the headpiece. I still can't believe you gave them to me."

"I removed them from your great-grandmother's wedding gown years ago after moths spoiled it." Estelle gave her niece a fond look. "I can imagine no better use for them."

"A few weeks ago I despaired of finishing my gown in time, but now I believe we'll make it. Only two weeks until my wedding!"

"Fifteen days until Christmas. Flora's gown is ready, and mine needs only the buttonholes."

Margie left the teapot to give her aunt a hug. "You were wonderful to sew Flora's gown, and I can't express how excited I am that you will come out of mourning for my wedding."

Estelle patted Margie's hand on her shoulder. "It has been more than six months since my mother's death."

"Yes, but—" Margie stopped and returned to preparing the tea.

"You've heard that I've worn mourning since my fiancé's death twenty years ago?"

The girl nodded hesitantly.

Estelle pursed her lips and flexed her fingers. "I no longer believe it necessary." Abruptly she picked up her pen and began to write again.

"Here's your tea, Auntie."

Estelle accepted the cup and saucer, meeting her niece's worried gaze. "Thank you, Marjorie."

"You're welcome. Why are you frowning? Did I offend you?" Margie sat across from Estelle and stirred her tea. "I'm sorry if I did."

81

"No, child. I was preoccupied."

"Thinking about Pastor Nelson?" Margie clinked her teacup into its saucer and leaned forward, resting her chin on her palm and her elbow on the table. "So are you going to marry him? David told me about his courting you. Pa doesn't seem to think you ought to marry him, but I think it would be wonderful! You'd be my mother-in-law, sort of. David says he's been afraid Pastor would let Mary Bilge bully him into marrying her, so he would be thrilled to have you as a stepmother instead."

"Mary Bilge?" Estelle nearly choked. "I hardly think so."

Margie covered her mouth. Her hazel eyes twinkled above the napkin.

"She must be several years his senior." The idea turned Estelle's stomach. "Do you think he might marry her if I turn him down?"

"I hope not! But David says she has turned into a decent cook and bought herself some new clothes. He suspects she's hunting for a husband, and her sights are set on Pastor. Have you seen her at church recently?"

"No. I am usually at the piano before and after services."

"She comes late and leaves early. But no matter how well she cooks or how much better she looks, she's not the woman for Pastor. I think she scares him."

Recalling how he had overlooked Mary's shoddy work, Estelle was inclined to agree. "I taught her to clean and cook," she said, staring blankly at the table. "I felt sorry for her. She resented me, but I had no idea. . ."

"You had no idea he would fall in love with you," Margie said.

Estelle knew her cheeks were flushing. "Nonsense."

Margie chuckled. "And I think you're in love with him, too, though you don't know it yet. How sweet!"

Estelle gathered up her papers and stacked them. "With your wedding date approaching, you are in a romantic state of mind. Reverend Nelson considers remarriage for purely practical reasons."

Smirking, Margie picked up the empty teacups and carried them to the sink.

Falling snow sparkled in the light of Frank's lantern as he hiked home from church one evening humming a Christmas carol. Snug beneath its white blanket, the parsonage welcomed him with a warm glow. He climbed over the buried gate and slogged to the front door. The path would require shoveling come morning, but not even that prospect could dim his joy.

Ever since Estelle had agreed to join him for the sleigh ride, his hopes had been high. Although he seldom spoke with her in private, her questions about his manuscript told him she was seeking God's truth. He needed only to be patient.

Smiling, he burst into song as he stepped into the entryway. "Glory to the newborn King. Peace on earth and—"

"Take off your boots. You're messing up my clean floor." Mary appeared in the kitchen doorway, wiping both hands on her apron.

"Oh, you're still here?" He stated the obvious.

"I baked you a chicken, and it ain't done yet," Mary said and pointed at his feet. "The boots."

After hanging up his coat and hat, he obediently used the bootjack, but his mind rebelled. It was time, past time, to put Mary back in her proper place. Lately she had taken to spending entire days in the parsonage, rearranging and. . .

He didn't know what else she did all day, but he knew it wasn't cleaning. The woman behaved as if she regarded his house as her domain.

He set his jaw and padded into the kitchen. Mary was removing a pan from the oven. As she straightened, he observed pleats across the expansive waist of her white apron. Navy skirts swept the floor, and iron-gray fluff surrounded her head. "What happened to your coat?"

Lines deepened around her mouth. "Got myself two new gowns and warshed my hair nigh on a month ago, and you just now noticed?" Her dark eyes skewered him with a glance.

He floundered for a proper response. "You look cleaner. Quite unobjectionable."

She grunted, sliced meat from the chicken, and slapped it on his plate. "Want preserves on your bread?"

"Please."

She jerked her head toward the cellar door. "Down cellar."

He blinked, then picked up a lamp, lifted the latch on the door, and descended into the clammy hole. Canned fruits and vegetables, gifts from parishioners, lined the wooden shelves protruding from the frozen sod walls. He found a jar of peach preserves and climbed back upstairs. After placing the jar on the table, he folded his arms. "Mary Bilge, it's past time you and I had a talk."

A wave of feminine emotion flitted across her face. She reached up to pat her hair into place. "Yes, Preacher?"

The quick changes in her attitude and expression confused Frank. One moment she was a bad-tempered harridan; the next moment she became an amiable woman.

"I pay you to fix my meals and clean my house, not to tell me what to do. I don't expect a slave, but I do require respect. If my future wife decides to retain your services around the house, you will need to give her the same measure of respect."

Only her trembling jowls revealed life.

"Mary, I don't want to seem ungrateful. . . ."

She turned around, picked up the pan holding the roast chicken, and dumped it upside down into the sink. Brandishing a wooden spoon, she approached Frank. He looked down into eyes like sparking flints.

"Next time I see that skinny icicle woman, I'll break her in half." With a loud crack, she snapped the spoon in two over her knee.

Stunned, Frank watched as Mary Bilge hauled on her tattered coat, hat, and overshoes and stumped outside through the kitchen door, leaving a rush of icy air in her wake.

Satin gowns in varied shades of blue were draped over armchairs around the parlor. Margie's gown enveloped the sofa, shimmering in snowy splendor. Susan stepped back and reviewed the finery once more. "We'll curl our hair before we leave home and hope the curl lasts until the ceremony. Estelle, I truly don't know how we would have managed without you."

Estelle rested in a rocking chair near the fireplace. "These months since I arrived in Iowa have been the best of my life. I'm grateful to be part of this family."

"My gown is glorious," Margie said, clasping her hands at her breast and closing her eyes. "I can scarcely wait until David sees me in it tomorrow!"

"And I can scarcely wait to see Auntie Stell in her new gown," Flora added. "We'll be twins." The girl wrapped one arm around Estelle's neck and leaned close. "And we'll be ever so beautiful."

Estelle kissed the child's soft cheek. "Beautiful we shall be, my dear. And humble, too."

Flora giggled. Tapping all ten fingers on a side table, she pretended to play the piano. "Wish I could play the wedding march tomorrow. I can play it really good. Can't I, Auntie Stell?"

"Indeed you do play well," Estelle said. "Your progress has been remarkable."

Susan smiled. "I imagine someday you'll play piano for many weddings, but not this one. Now off to bed, Flora. Tomorrow will be a busy day."

"And the next day is Christmas!" Flora exclaimed. "I hope it snows more and more. Joshua promised I could ride with him for the Christmas sleigh ride this year."

"Oh, did he?" Susan accepted her daughter's good-night kiss.

"He says this year I'm his best girl, and I'm light, so he'll win all the races."

"Ah, the truth comes out." Margie laughed. "Josh is determined to beat Abel Coon this year."

Flora skipped into the hall and thumped upstairs.

Paul entered through the front door in a gust of frigid wind, brushing fresh snow from his shoulders. His ladies shooed him away from the satin.

"I hope it doesn't storm tomorrow," Margie said, her face clouding. "Any other year I would be thrilled at the prospect of snow for Christmas Eve, but not now. People might not be able to come to my wedding if the weather is bad."

"All you really need is a minister and a groom."

"Papa!" Margie protested.

Paul chuckled. "Last night at home for our girl." He hugged Margie, blinked hard, and cleared his throat. "Best get some sleep, all of you. I'm heading up to bed."

"You're right, Papa. Good night, Mama. Good night, Auntie Stell." Margie followed her sister and her father upstairs.

Susan took Margie's empty chair. "It seems like a

dream. My little girl will be married tomorrow."

"She'll make a good wife for David. She took me to see her house last week. Such a lovely home it will be." Estelle gazed into the fire.

"You needn't envy her, Estelle. You'll make the parsonage into a lovely home, I imagine."

Estelle fanned her face. She had never been one to blush, but everything seemed different since her arrival in Iowa. "I never intended to marry."

"I believe Frank never intended to remarry, but then he met you. And tasted your cooking."

Estelle met Susan's twinkling gaze. "You believe he wishes to marry me for practical reasons."

Susan laughed aloud. "Not for a moment. He loves you, Estelle."

"I understand practical. I don't understand love."

Susan stared into the fire and spoke in dreamy tones. "Does anyone understand love? Why do I love Paul? Sometimes he annoys me; often I irritate him. Yet we are devoted to each other. God calls Christians to demonstrate love to one another whether we wish to or not. The amazing thing is that feelings often follow actions. I was afraid to love you when you first arrived here, Estelle. Yet I resolved to demonstrate God's love to you, and to my surprise, I grew to love you dearly."

Estelle listened in silent amazement.

"Love is perilous," Susan continued. "God knows this better than anyone, for He loves most. At Christmas we celebrate His greatest risk of all. When I think of God the Almighty lying in a manger as a helpless baby, the chance He took for the sake of love quite steals my breath away."

"Chance? God?"

"Yes, chance. For love of you, Estelle, He was mocked, beaten, and brutally killed. Then He conquered death and sin and returned to heaven to prepare a beautiful home for you. He could force you to love Him in return; He has enough power to make you do anything He wants you to do. But He doesn't desire the love of a puppet, so He simply woos you as a lover and longs for you to return His love."

Susan's words burned into Estelle's soul like a hot iron. The pain finally propelled her out of the chair and upstairs, where she lay in bed and shivered for hours.

Chapter 7

Estelle smoothed a calico apron over the skirts of her blue satin gown and glanced around at the other women working to decorate the hotel dining room. Frank's parishioners had leaped at the chance to help prepare the wedding reception for their minister's son. Of course, many of these women had known Margie since her birth. Estelle found the townsfolk's loyalty appealing.

Of particular interest to Estelle was the plump, golden-haired young woman helping Susan arrange table centerpieces—Amy Nelson Syverson. Amy had greeted Estelle earlier with a twinkle in her blue eyes. She must know about her father's intent to remarry, and apparently she approved. The knowledge boosted Estelle's spirits.

Entering the kitchen to see if she could be useful, she

discovered several ladies in a huddle. Their concerned expressions roused her curiosity. "Is anything wrong?"

"Nothing serious," Mrs. Isobel Coon said. "We need a few more jars of fruit for an after-dinner sweet, but I suppose we can stretch what we have here to feed fifty people. If only Loretta hadn't broken—"

"Plenty of fruit in the parsonage cellar."

Estelle recognized that gruff voice. Mary Bilge stood at the huge cast-iron stove, stirring a pot, the old slouch hat pulled down over her eyes. Her change in clothing style had been short-lived.

Mrs. Coon nodded. "Pastor Nelson is probably at the church already, but I'm sure he'd be willing to donate fruit for his son's wedding reception. And the parsonage is just down the street. Where is Amy? Someone ask her to fetch us a few jars of peaches or pears."

Mrs. Fallbrook shook her head. "I saw her and Susan leave. Mary Bilge, would you—"

"No." Mary turned her broad back.

The other ladies blinked at each other, obviously trying to remain pleasant. "Well then, I suppose we must do without." They bustled off to finish their preparations.

Estelle approached Mary. "I can stir that soup while you get the fruit. It'd be a shame to run short of food at David and Margie's wedding reception."

"La-de-da. If you want it, you get it."

Her lips tightening, Estelle nodded. "Very well. I shall. Tell the others where I've gone." She hung her apron on a hook and located her cloak and overshoes. She would have to hurry. Josh had promised to stop by and pick her up on his way to the church.

Estelle left the hotel by the side door closest to the parsonage. A light snow frosted her woolen cloak, but she was able to keep her skirts hoisted above the drifts lining the street. If her new gown became soiled before the wedding, she would never forgive Mary Bilge. The selfish woman! What had gotten into her lately? She seemed like the old Mary again, even smelling of cigar smoke.

Frank must have shoveled his walk that morning. The front steps were icy but clear. It seemed strange to enter the parsonage uninvited. Belle greeted her in the hallway. "So you are lady of the house today?" Estelle stooped to stroke the cat. A mildew odor from the rug told her that Mary's housekeeping enthusiasm had waned along with her personal cleanliness. Poor Frank.

The kitchen was warm and smelled of something burnt. Restraining her urge to tidy up, Estelle peeled off her gloves and lit a candle at the oven's banked coals. She lifted the wooden latch on the cellar door and stared down into darkness. Stale, frigid air wafted up the steps.

"You stay up here, Belle. I don't want to accidentally shut you in. I'll be only a moment."

Her shoes clopped on the wooden risers as she descended into the hole, keeping her skirts from brushing the whitewashed earth wall. Shivering, she scanned the shelves and located two jars of spiced peaches and one of pears. To carry three quart jars and a candle while safeguarding her gown would be impractical, so she hunted for a tote basket. Candle lifted high, she spotted a dusty one on the end of a top shelf.

Just as she reached for it, something banged up in the kitchen and Belle let out a yowl. Dust sifted through between the boards overhead. At that moment, the cellar door shut and the candle extinguished. Estelle spun about and heard the thunk of the latch dropping into place.

"Oh, no!"

Above, the floorboards creaked, and Belle meowed. Maybe the cat had bumped the door, causing it to close. Feeling her way in the darkness, Estelle hefted her skirts and climbed the wooden steps. She pushed at the unyielding door, then felt for the latchstring. It was missing. A cat would not have pulled it through to the other side.

Someone had shut her in the cellar. Mary Bilge was the only person who knew she had come for the fruit.

Mary must have done it. But why? What could she hope to gain by such a petty, senseless act?

Rubbing her upper arms, Estelle sat on the second step down. At least she still wore her woolen cloak. Her gloves lay on the kitchen table, and her overshoes were near the front door. Frank would surely find her soon.

Something furry touched her hand, and she yelped. A mouse? The something scrabbled at the door and gave a soft meow.

Estelle relaxed. "Belle?" She felt along the crack beneath the door and found a paw. The cat was reaching for her. "You scared me." Estelle slid her fingers through the opening and touched a warm, vibrating body, a shadow against the dim slit of light visible beneath the door. *At least I'm not entirely alone. Someone will come after me before the wedding starts. They need me to play the piano.*

She tucked her feet in close and huddled beneath her cloak, resting her cheek against the solid door. "It's cold down here, but I'm sure Frank will find me before I freeze to death, and you're here to keep my fingers warm, Belle. Why would Mary lock me in the cellar? The person she hurts most by doing this is poor Marjorie, who will have no music for her wedding if they don't find me soon." Her voice sounded thin.

Long minutes passed. Aside from Belle's occasional

mew and rumbling purr, Estelle heard only her own thoughts. She considered calling for help, but who would hear? The cellar had no windows.

She tried to estimate the amount of time passing. The gray slit beneath the door finally vanished. Would they go ahead with the wedding? She pictured Margie in her gown, gazing up into David's adoring eyes. How lovely the bride would be, and how handsome her young groom!

Trying to ignore the cold, she hummed the wedding march. Outside, snow would sparkle in the lantern light, turning Coon's Hollow into a Christmas wonderland. At the wedding there would be laughter and rejoicing, yet for Estelle the night was silent.

"Why did You allow me to miss Margie's wedding, God?" Despite her disappointment, she couldn't rouse herself to anger. Her recent studies of God's ways and His nature assured her that He allowed nothing to happen without reason. Oddly enough, her soul felt peaceful as her thoughts drifted back over last night's chat with Susan.

"Lately it does seem that every conversation, every argument circles back to the subject of love. Your love for me and my lack of love for others." She spoke just above a whisper. "I arrived here in the heat and light of summer, yet my heart was colder than ice. Now I sit in frozen darkness and feel the warmth of Your love. Your presence, not my circumstances, makes the difference."

Music wafted through her thoughts, and she began to hum, then sing quietly. "Silent night, holy night. Son of God, Love's pure light." She hummed again, pondering the words. "All these years I have denied Your love. I struggled alone in despair when I might have rejoiced daily in the knowledge of You. Because my parents failed me, Paul left, and John died, I quit believing. You offered to share my burdens and ease my load, but I refused You."

Tears welled up in Estelle's eyes, overflowed, and burned her cheeks. "It's not too late for me, is it, Lord? I acknowledge my hopeless condition; without You I am nothing—a selfish, cold, meaningless woman. Love is painful—You know that better than anyone—but I want to live and love and hurt along with You. Forgive my anger and my unbelief, and truly be Lord of my life."

The walls of ice split apart and crashed into the sea of God's love. The floodgates of Estelle's soul opened wide, sweeping away every icicle of bitterness and anger and filling her with living water. For the first time in more than twenty years, she wept cleansing tears of joy.

She must have slept, for the next thing Estelle knew, the door swung away and Frank lifted her into his arms.

Still groggy, she felt his brushy beard against her cheek. He trembled as if he were cold, yet his embrace enveloped her in warmth. She rested her face on his waistcoat and patted his shoulder. "Dear Frank, is the wedding over?"

"How on earth did you get shut in there?" he asked, his voice breaking. "We've been looking everywhere for you! I knew something must be wrong when you didn't show up for the wedding, but I waited until after the ceremony to panic. How did you end up in my cellar?" He sat on a kitchen chair and settled her on his lap, rocking her like a child. His big hands pressed her to his chest, stroked her face, tucked her cloak around her, then hugged her again as if he could never bring her close enough.

Light from the lamp on the table glowed in Belle's golden eyes. A moment later the cat leaped into Estelle's lap to join the embrace. "Belle kept me company and warmed my fingers." Estelle tucked a fold of her cloak around the purring cat.

Worry still vibrated in Frank's voice. "I've got to let Paul know you're safe. First tell me what happened. Josh feels terrible; he was supposed to pick you up at the hotel, but when he arrived there, you were already gone."

Estelle told her short tale. "Mary Bilge is the only one who knew where I went. I suspect she shut me in the cellar, but, Frank, please don't confront her about it."

"Why ever not?" His eyes blazed in the lamplight. "You might have frozen to death down there!" He smoothed hair from her temple, and she felt his fingers shaking.

"Nonsense. It isn't that cold, and I'm sure Mary expected you to find me today. Her conduct was spiteful and childish, not vicious," Estelle said. "But poor Margie! Did she walk down the aisle in silence?"

To her surprise, Frank chuckled. "No. Your prize piano student played the wedding march with more animation than accuracy."

"Flora?" Estelle sat up straight.

"Yes, Flora. The child performed well, and Margie seemed as happy as any new bride despite the lack of refinement in her accompaniment."

Estelle laughed aloud. "I would almost suspect Flora of shutting me into the cellar, if she'd had any opportunity. The little sprite undoubtedly enjoyed her chance to shine."

Frank stared.

Estelle touched her face, wondering if she had smeared dirt on her cheek or nose. "What is wrong?"

"I've never heard you laugh before."

Suddenly conscious of her position on his lap, Estelle

pulled away and rose. Belle squawked in complaint and jumped to the floor. "Would you like a cup of tea? I need something warm to drink."

"No, thank you."

She moved the kettle over the heat. "I must tell you something, Frank. You deserve to know."

He looked wary. "I'm listening."

Estelle busied her hands with setting out a teacup. "Although I'm sorry I missed the wedding, I believe the Lord wanted time alone with me."

When she looked up, surprise lit Frank's features. She glanced away, still trying to control her emotions, yet her voice trembled. "I finally understand about love."

"You do?"

A smile broke free and spread across her face. "Oh, Frank, how much I have missed all these years! You tried to explain, but only God could reveal the wonder of His love. I know I can never make up for the years I've wasted, but all the life I have left belongs to the Lord."

He covered his face with both hands. Emotion clogged his deep voice. "I'm so glad, Estelle. So glad." He pulled a handkerchief from his jacket pocket and mopped his eyes, avoiding her gaze.

Her hands formed fists. She hid them behind her back, sucked in a deep breath, and took the plunge. "I would gladly spend the rest of my life with you, Frank Nelson."

He pushed back his chair and arose but remained at the table. "No more anger?"

She shook her head.

"No more fear?"

"Actually, I'm terrified." Her legs would give out at any moment.

He sounded short of breath. "So am I. Dearest Estelle, are you certain you can endure living in this tiny old parsonage with a rustic boor of a minister? You're so genteel and elegant, and I feel like a buffalo around you sometimes. I know my loud voice annoys you, and I leave my clothes lying around and forget to change into a clean shirt or polish my boots. . ."

Estelle dared to look at his face. "Then you need me to remind you. I want to feel needed. The happiest days of my life were the days I spent caring for your home and preparing meals for you. I shall try to be gentle and meek instead of bossy and high-handed."

"And I shall endeavor to be considerate." He folded his arms across his great chest. "Often you remind me of Belle, the way she demands affection only on her terms."

Estelle translated his unspoken question. "You fear angering me with unwelcome attentions?"

He slowly nodded.

She lowered her gaze and pondered the matter. "I have never possessed a demonstrative nature, and adjusting to the demands of marriage may require time. If you can be patient, I shall accustom myself to fulfilling your needs." Her face grew hot.

"I promise the same to you. And now, much though I hate to end this moment, we must consider the needs of our family and friends and assure them all of your safety."

Estelle lost interest in tea. She moved the kettle off the stovetop. "I have no idea what time it is. Are we too late for the wedding reception?"

"Not at all. The wedding ended less than an hour ago. The food should be hot and plentiful. Let's join the guests at the hotel and announce our own news." He paused, and his brows suddenly drew together. "We do have news, don't we? You will marry me?"

Estelle smiled. "I shall."

His face beamed like a summer sunrise. "I confess I jumped the gun and told Amy about my hopes. She seems to approve of my choice."

"I suspected as much; she was particularly friendly to me. A lovely young woman, Frank."

"I think so." He glowed with pride.

Estelle drew on her gloves. "I hope Paul approves. I know Susan will. Oh! We mustn't forget the three jars of fruit."

"I'll fetch them. You stay out of that cellar until I fit it with a modern doorknob that doesn't lock." Frank tapped her cheek with one finger. His eyes caught her gaze and held. "I love you, Estelle."

"Frank," she whispered, then found herself wrapped in a mighty hug. Her arms slid around him, and she pressed her cheek to his chest. His hand cupped her head, destroying her hairstyle, but she didn't care.

Chapter 8

Christmas morning dawned clear and bright. "No wind yet," Josh announced as the men came in from chores for breakfast, red-cheeked and stamping snow from their boots. "It's a perfect day for a sleigh ride."

Flora squealed and danced a little jig with Eliza frisking around her skirts. "Did you see what St. Nicholas put in my stocking, Josh? An orange, and horehound candy, a penny, and a little doll with a real china head!"

Estelle smiled as she set a dish of fried potatoes on the table. She had purchased the doll head at a shop in Madison many years earlier, unable to resist its sanguine smile. Together she and Susan had completed the doll for Flora and created its miniature wardrobe.

Joe played with his new gyroscope until Paul reminded

him that the breakfast table was an improper place for toys. Joe hid it beneath the tablecloth. "Did this really belong to you when you were my age, Pa?"

"It did. Your aunt saved it all these years and brought it for you."

"Thank you, Auntie Stell."

"You're most welcome." Estelle basked in her nephew's approval and his first use of her pet name. She sat beside Susan and passed dishes of food to the other ravenous young men. Not even Margie's empty place at the table caused sadness this glorious Christmas morning. Estelle imagined the young bride preparing breakfast for her young husband at their new home and smiled with satisfaction.

She met her brother's gaze. Paul reached over and grasped her hand. That one gesture expressed his forgiveness and acceptance. Her voice held a sister's lifetime love. "Merry Christmas, Paulie."

"And a blessed Christmas to you, Stell. Having you in our home and full of joy is the best gift I could receive today, I think." After one last squeeze of her fingers, he returned his attention to his breakfast. Noting his heightened color, Estelle let the emotional moment end.

Josh advised Flora to hurry if she still wanted to accompany him on the sleigh ride. Glowing with excitement, the little girl raced through her chores and ran upstairs. Estelle wondered when Frank would arrive. As soon as the kitchen was tidy, she did some primping of her own.

Along with the blue satin gown for Margie's wedding, Estelle had found time to add two new shirtwaists to her wardrobe, one white and one of gray calico with pink sprigs. They would enliven her worn black skirts and jackets until she found time and means to sew more colorful garments.

Regarding her reflection in the small mirror above the dressing table in her dormer bedroom, Estelle coaxed the wisps of hair behind her ears into loose curls. The mere memory of Frank's expression when she removed her cloak at the hotel last night brought a smile to her face. He found her attractive, she knew, and the realization pleased her beyond measure.

At the reception, he had kept her at his side throughout the evening. The most disturbing moment for Estelle had come when she met Mary Bilge's flinty stare. *That poor woman! Something must be done to help her. But what?* She was no worse off than Estelle had been upon her arrival in Coon's Hollow. God could bring joy and love into Mary's life, too, if she would allow it. With a nod at the mirror, Estelle appointed herself to pray for Miss Mary Bilge.

The pin-tucked white shirtwaist Estelle wore contrasted nicely with her black jacket, and a red ribbon at her throat gave it a festive touch. Hearing sleigh bells, she ran to the window. Powder trotted up the drive, blowing twin plumes of steam.

Lest she keep Frank waiting, Estelle hurried downstairs, tying a long scarf over her bonnet and tucking it around her throat. With the addition of her cloak, mittens, and overshoes, she considered herself ready to brave the weather. "Frank is here," she called, patting Eliza's silky black head.

"Enjoy yourself, dear," Susan answered from the kitchen.

Paul leaned against the kitchen doorframe. "Be home before dark," he warned with a twinkle.

"Yes, sir." Estelle gave him a hasty kiss before bustling outside.

Frank tucked her beneath robes and furs, climbed in beside her, and clucked to his horse. "Can't keep Powder standing when he's warm." At first the horse kicked up a frozen spray, but once he settled into his stride, Estelle uncovered her face.

"How beautiful!" Sunlight glittered on rolling drifts of pristine white. Silvery bells jingled with Powder's steady trot. The cold tingled her cheeks and froze inside her nose.

Frank's eyes seemed to reflect the vivid sky as he returned her smile. "Yes, you are beautiful."

Estelle unburied her arm enough to link it with his, then leaned her face against his shoulder. "This is the happiest day of my life."

"So far," he said with a grin. "I passed Josh and Flora on my way."

"They're off to the races, no doubt. I think Flora will be the envy of every eligible young woman in the county. I wonder why Josh hasn't started courting a girl yet," Estelle said.

"I imagine he hasn't found the right one," Frank answered. "I'm glad I waited until you came along."

Estelle snuggled closer. "I approve of your hat. It matches your eyes."

"So I was told by the lady who knitted it for me."

"Lady?"

He chuckled. "Jealous? Beatrice Coon was the lady."

The cutter swept through town, around on a looping county road, then back toward the Truman farm. Estelle waved at each sleigh they passed, recognizing chapped and smiling faces. David and Margie waved a joyous greeting but didn't pause to chat. Josh and Flora stopped to visit. Their horses pranced in place, steaming with sweat but still raring to go.

"I'm guessing by your smiles that you whipped Abel Coon today," Frank called.

"We beat him by a mile!" Flora shouted back. "But Abel says Josh cheated because I'm his sister and can't be his best girl."

Josh grinned. "He thought up that rule too late to do him any good this year."

Frank laughed. "Are you on your way home?"

"Yup. Got to give Chester and Sandy a good rubdown and some hot mash. They earned it today. Merry Christmas, and congratulations, Pastor Nelson. My aunt will make you a great wife." Josh winked at Estelle and clucked to his fretting horses.

"Good-bye," Flora called, and Estelle blew her a kiss.

Frank jiggled his reins, and Powder trotted on. "Amy and Bradley chose to remain at the parsonage today," Frank said. "Their best gift to me this year was the news that I'm to become a grandfather next summer. I hope you don't mind marrying a grandfather."

Despite his teasing tone, Estelle detected a hint of anxiety underlying his question. "As long as I get to be a stepgrandmother, I favor the idea. I love babies. Since I can never have a child of my own, I shall treasure the opportunity to love your children and grandchildren."

Powder slowed to a walk. Estelle studied their

surroundings. "Where are we?"

"Nowhere. I've been thinking and planning, but for the life of me I can't think of a place we could go today to find some privacy." Leaving his horse to set a moderate pace, Frank turned on the seat, caught her mittened hands, and brought them to his chest.

Estelle's heart thundered in her ears. Frost glittered in his eyebrows and mustache, but his expression warmed her face. His voice wavered. "This is our first Christmas together, and I want you to remember it always with joy." For a long moment, his blue eyes studied her. She saw his lips twitch with emotion and suddenly understood.

"I shall." She was too bundled up to move, so she put one hand behind his head and gently pulled his face toward hers. His frosty mustache tickled, but his lips on hers were surprisingly warm.

He sat back with a pleased smile. "Thank you."

"I love you, Frank."

His smile widened. Giving a little whoop, he snapped the reins and started his stalled horse off at a brisk trot.

Jill Stengl lives with her husband, Dean, and their family in the Northwoods of Wisconsin. They have four children and a busy life—Tom is an Air Force Academy cadet, Anne is in college, Jim is in high school, and Peter is Jill's last homeschool student. Jill loves to write books about exciting times, historic places, and unusual people—and animals somehow sneak their way into most of her stories. Her goal, one of these snowy winters, is to take a real sleigh ride!

Readers may contact Jill at jpopcorn@newnorth.net.

Take Me Home

by Tracey V. Bateman

Dedication

To my sister, Linda Devine.
I love you dearly.

Chapter 1

Coon's Hollow, Iowa—1887

A frigid wind assaulted Kathleen Johnson the second she stepped off the train onto the boardwalk in front of the Coon's Hollow station. A shiver began at the base of her spine and worked its way to a full-bodied shudder. Apparently Pa's prediction of an unusually frigid winter was coming true. Here it was barely mid-October and the gray clouds overhead seemed suspiciously plump. She wouldn't be surprised if it snowed overnight. Gripping her valise tight with one hand, she pulled her scarf closer about her head with the other and braved the few feet of cold wind until she reached the depot.

The smell of sawdust hung in the air, tickling her nose

and throat. She gave a little cough and glanced about, looking for someone who might be looking for her. The telegram from Reverend Nelson had promised that someone would be at the station to collect her upon her arrival. But though she received numerous curious glances, no one seemed inclined to offer her a ride.

With a sigh, she made her way to the ticket booth and placed a gloved hand on the tall counter. "Excuse me, please."

The man glanced up. His brow rose, and his face split into a leer at the sight of her. "Well, well. How can I help you, little lady?"

Barely containing her revulsion at the lecherous tone, she swallowed hard, wishing that Pa or one of her four brothers were here to put this man in his place. The fact that she was on her own now for the first time ever washed over her with startling clarity.

She forced the deepest frown she could muster and raised her chin. "I am looking for someone—"

"Look no farther, beautiful girl," he shot back, his eyes traveling over her face and neck. Kathleen had never been more grateful for her petite height, which in this instance kept everything below her shoulders hidden from his view.

"No, I'm not looking for someone like that." Her face

burned, and she wished she could think of a crushing retort, thereby reducing his cocky exterior to a puddle of shame. But as usual, when faced with conflict, words failed her.

He leaned on the counter, his elbow supporting him. His hand shot out and covered hers before she could anticipate the move and pull back. "Don't break my heart, honey. I'm looking for someone just like you."

A gasp escaped her lips at his boldness, and she snatched her hand away. He was bordering on more than rudeness. Before she could conjure a thought, rescue came in the form of a puff of smoke and a declaration. "Abel Coon, I've half a mind to tell your pa what I just overheard. Bet your ma'd beat the tar outta ya, iffen she was still kickin', God rest her soul."

"Mind your own business." The man scowled over Kathleen's shoulder.

Kathleen whipped around and nearly passed out at the sight of her savior. The woman—at least she guessed it was a woman—wore a man's overcoat that hung open, revealing an ill-fitting brown dress. A fat cigar hung from thin lips, and a wide-brimmed hat rested on her mop of gray hair. Her broad forehead and large nose made her look rather masculine, and sagging jowls reminded Kathleen of her family's bulldog, Toby.

Abel gave a loud, pointed cough. "No smoking in the depot, Mary."

"It'll take someone a lot tougher than you to stop me, you little pip-squeak."

Though Kathleen was a bit taken aback by Mary's habit as well, she couldn't help but be glad the woman didn't obey the despicable flirt behind the counter.

Mary snatched the cigar from her lips and held it between her fingers as she sized Kathleen up. "You the new teacher?"

"Yes, ma'am."

"Thought so." She gave a curt nod. "The reverend sent me to take you over to the school, though why I do favors for the likes of him. . ."

Relief coursed through Kathleen. "Oh, thank you, Mrs. . ."

Without asking, the woman reached out and took Kathleen's valise. "*Miss* Bilge, for now."

"Oh, are you soon to be wed, Miss Bilge?"

Abel's laughter echoed through the station. "In a pig's eye."

Miss Bilge's manly face turned scarlet, and she scowled at the ill-mannered young man. "Shut up, Abel. I don't see no gals takin' you up on any offers lately."

He reddened, and Mary Bilge nodded her satisfaction

as she turned her attention back to Kathleen. "I ain't engaged, formally. But that don't mean I ain't willin' if the right fella came along. That's why I said I'm a *miss* for now."

"I see." Bewildered, Kathleen left her response there. Fortunately, Miss Bilge seemed ready to move on. She glanced about the floor, then looked back to Kathleen. "This your only bag?"

"Yes, ma'am."

She gave a loud snort, adding to her already unlady-like demeanor. "Must not be plannin' to stay very long."

Kathleen once again felt her cheeks grow warm. "Well, I was. . ." What could she say? The astute lady was pretty much right. Her presence in Coon's Hollow was a trial run. First time teaching. First time away from home. Biting her lip, she fought the approach of hot tears.

Thankfully, Miss Bilge nodded in understanding, making it unnecessary for Kathleen to elaborate. "Ya want to make sure a town like Coon's Hollow is where you want to hang your hat permanently before you bring anything more than can fit in this here bag? Can't say as I blame a young thing like you. The last gal barely stayed a month."

Well, that explained the need for a quick replace-ment. The head of the Rosewood school board happened to be brothers with a member of Coon's Hollow's school board. Coon's Hollow had need of a teacher to fill in for the rest of the term. Kathleen's father, who sat on the Rosewood school board, had approached her with the suggestion. Though she hated the thought, she'd agreed to take the teacher's exam and left the results in God's hands. Two weeks later, here she was, shaking from head to toe from nerves and cold, feeling for all she was worth as though she'd bitten off more than she could chew in a million years.

Kathleen swallowed hard as Miss Bilge tossed her valise into the back of a wagon and offered her a hand up.

"Thank you."

The woman walked around to the other side of the wagon and swung herself up, forcing Kathleen to avert her gaze at the flash of a hairy calf as the patched skirt hiked. "Oops." Mary sent her an embarrassed grin and quickly righted her skirt. Kathleen couldn't help but return the smile.

Slapping the reins, Miss Bilge nodded in approval. "You'll do just fine. Don't worry about that Abel Coon. He's all talk. I'm thinking his pa regrets ever teaching him to speak."

Gathering all the bravado she could muster, Kathleen sat up a little straighter. "He didn't bother me. I was just about to put him in his place when you walked up."

"Sure you were. But I'm right proud of you for trying to be brave." She waved to a passerby. "The last gal nearly fainted every time she saw a mouse."

"M—mouse?"

"You scared of those furry little critters, too?"

Kathleen cleared her throat. "I should say not." She should say *so*! "A—are there any in the teacherage?"

"Tons of 'em. They come in from the field out back of the building. But don't worry. They ain't gonna hurt you. Just trying to get out of the cold."

Kathleen shivered as the wind whipped up and shook the wagon. "Well, I certainly can't blame them for that. I wouldn't mind getting out of this cold myself. Are we almost there?"

"It's just at the edge of town."

Kathleen followed the point of Miss Bilge's cigar. Her heart sank as she observed the clapboard structure. She'd expected a whitewashed building with a bell and a porch, like the school in Rosewood. She was sorely disappointed. The roof was straight across over one portion of the building, then slanted downward as though in an afterthought another room had been added. She assumed the afterthought would be her quarters.

Another gust of wind shook the structure, and Kathleen felt her spirits plummet further. It must be

121

freezing inside with walls so thin. How would she ever stay warm? And it was only October. The term ended in two months, so she'd be home for Christmas. She could be brave that long. She hoped.

"Looks like someone built a fire." Miss Bilge's gruff voice broke through Kathleen's thoughts.

"Huh?"

"There's smoke comin' from the chimney."

"Oh, that's a mercy. My fingers are nearly frozen off."

The woman chuckled as she halted the team and hopped down. After wrapping the reins around the hitching post, she grabbed Kathleen's bag from the back. Kathleen stared. "Need help getting down?" the woman asked.

Heat warmed her cheeks. "I–I can do it."

She climbed down, careful to keep her skirt covering her legs. She stumbled a little as she touched the ground. Kathleen gathered her composure and followed Miss Bilge, who was almost to the door.

Suddenly, she was very glad that she'd decided against bringing a trunk. She'd already made up her mind. Coon's Hollow wasn't the town for her. She most definitely would not be accepting a certificate for another term. Lecherous train station men, crazy women who looked and talked more like men, mice in the schoolhouse. She shuddered.

How she wished she'd never agreed to this venture. Mama had warned her that she'd regret it, and as usual, Mama was right. Why had she ever listened to Caleb? Her favorite brother had been wrong in this instance. "Kat," he'd said. "Don't make the same mistake I did. You might find that you don't want to stay in Rosewood forever." At her gasp, he'd hurried on. "Now, don't think I'm not happy with Deborah and my girls, because I am. But maybe I would have liked the chance to make a choice. You have that chance. Take it."

And against her better judgment, Kathleen had taken his advice. Now she missed her family so fiercely it was all she could do to keep herself from bursting into tears. Though they'd said good-bye only this morning, her stomach tightened at the thought of them. Ma would be starting to fix supper, and the two younger boys would be finishing up chores while the two older boys helped Pa in the family-owned livery stable.

"Ya comin', gal?"

Kathleen jerked her gaze from the frigid ground to find Miss Bilge filling the doorway, her cigar a mere stub between her lips.

"Yes, I'm coming."

"It ain't much to look at, but we can get it fixed up in no time."

Kathleen couldn't stifle a gasp at her first sight of the schoolhouse. Every desk, including hers, was overturned, and many were broken. Dirt and mice droppings layered the floor, along with scattered books and tablets.

"What on earth happened?"

"Ain't no tellin'. My guess is a pack of ornery young 'uns with too much time on their hands since there ain't been no school. You can straighten 'em out in no time."

A sigh pushed from Kathleen's lungs. She would need at least a week to ready this room for school, and how would she ever control a group of students who were rowdy enough to cause this sort of damage?

Miss Bilge clucked her tongue and snatched up her valise once more. "Come on, gal."

"Wh–where are we going?"

"Back to the train station. This town ain't for the likes of you."

Chapter 2

At his first sight of the new teacher, Josh Truman nearly dropped the armload of wood he carried. He gaped at the young woman who followed quickly behind Mary Bilge, taking two steps to every one of the older lady's.

The teacher reached forward and took hold of Mary's arm. "Miss Bilge, please wait. I haven't said I want to go back."

A puff of wind caught the teacher's scarf, pushing it back from her face. Josh caught a glimpse of a lovely rounded face and enormous blue eyes. He sucked in a breath and tried to remember where he was. She reminded him of one of those store-bought dolls that Auntie Stell had brought back for his little sister, Flora, when she and the preacher returned from their honeymoon last summer.

Only this living, breathing doll was a lot prettier.

He blinked. They sure hadn't made teachers like that when he went to school. As a matter of fact, most of his instructors looked more like Miss Bilge. Except they were all men.

He smiled at his own joke, then frowned as he realized the two women were moving away from the school rather than toward it. Where did that crazy Mary think she was taking the new schoolteacher? "Hey, where are you going?"

Mary snatched her trademark cigar from her mouth and tossed it to the ground, crushing it beneath the toe of her clunky men's boot. "New record for shortest time a teacher stayed. Looks like Wayne Sharpton wins the bet. He said Miss Johnson here would take one look at the schoolroom and hightail it home."

"Bet?" The young teacher's voice squeaked, and she stopped dead in her tracks. "Everyone's gambling about me? But that's. . .that's sinful. Besides, I never said. . ."

Feeling like he'd been kicked in the gut by her distress, Josh hurried to reassure her. "No, miss. Not everyone. Only the most disreputable characters in town."

Mary drew herself up and pinned him with a scowl fierce enough to scare a mama bear away from her cub. "There ain't no call to be insultin'."

Warmth flooded Josh's cheeks. "Sorry, Miss Bilge."

With a disgruntled snort, she hefted the valise she carried to the back of the wagon. "Not as sorry as I am. I lost two bits to that Wayne Sharpton." She shook her head in obvious disgust. "I gotta give up gamblin' on these teachers 'fore I end up in the poorhouse. I figured this one would stay for sure. Just had me a feelin'."

Miss Johnson gathered her dignity and squared her shoulders. "Pardon me for being the cause of your debt, Miss Bilge."

The young woman's offense was lost on Mary. "Debt? Naw, this is cash on the barrel. No one can bet lessen they got the money right then."

"Oh. Well, anyway, I never said I wanted to leave."

Mary squinted. "Don't ya? I thought sure it was all over for ya the second ya saw that wrecked building."

The young teacher hesitated. "While I admit I was a bit taken aback, I am not so easily deterred. I promised my father and the school board that I would teach until the end of the term."

Josh's heart soared. "Bravo, Miss Johnson."

Her eyes widened, and a dimple flashed in her cheek, sending his heart racing faster than at a log-splitting contest. "Thank you," she said, her tone velvety soft.

By the time he found his voice, she touched him

lightly on the arm, and he lost it again.

She focused those beautiful, ocean blue eyes on him, nodding toward the wood in his arms. "Are you the one who built the fire in the schoolhouse?"

Josh nodded. "I was just about to go inside and start cleaning up the mess. I'd be honored if you'd allow me to continue with my plan and help get the room ready for classes." He hesitated. "Unless, of course, you've decided not to stay in Coon's Hollow."

"That's very kind of you." She turned to Mary and smiled. "Miss Bilge, I despise gambling as the devil's sport; however, you may just win that bet after all."

Soapy water sloshed onto the plank floor as Kathleen pushed the bucket forward, then crawled after it to the next filthy spot in the room. Mary Bilge lit another cigar—her second in an hour—and stared at Kathleen, her lined face scrunching together as she appeared to be pondering.

Kathleen's face flooded with warmth. She knew the woman suspected that her quick turnabout was in response to Josh's presence. But that wasn't true. The least she could do was stay after the generous man had given of his time to chop firewood and offer to clean.

Besides, it wasn't her idea to go back home in the first place, and she had been trying to tell Miss Bilge that very thing when Josh showed up.

Her reason for staying had nothing whatsoever to do with Mr. Josh Truman or his lovely brown eyes that reminded her so much of the dark trunk of the maple tree in her backyard. After all, she had no interest in courting a young man from another county. Mama would just about die if she even considered it. All five of the Johnson children knew they were expected to stay in or around Rosewood when they married, and of the two that were married already, they had, without fail, obeyed. Pa joked that Mama's expectation was similar to God instructing the children of Israel—absolutely no foreign marriages. Mama's word was law in their household.

Another puff of smoke wafted into the air, pulling Kathleen from her thoughts.

"Miss Bilge, things might go much faster if you'd consider lending your assistance." Kathleen hated to be rude, but the woman was making her nervous as she watched and smoked and made silent assumptions.

"Well, la-de-da, missy. I ain't here to work; I'm here to chaperone. If I get myself too wrapped up in cleanin', I might miss something between you two young people."

Kathleen's cheeks warmed. "I assure you, Miss Bilge,

you have no need to concern yourself about that. I've no intention of allowing anything between Mr. Truman and myself."

"That so?" The skepticism in her tone grated on Kathleen.

"Yes, it most certainly is."

"Then how come your voice changed when you spoke to young Josh? And how come you flashed those dimples when you smiled at him? And how come—"

"Why, I did no such thing." Only outrage could have caused her to rudely interrupt her elder, but Kathleen refused to stand by and be falsely accused of. . .flirting.

"Did too." Mary's cigar hung from her mouth as she folded her arms across her chest, stubbornly making a stand for what she believed.

"Okay, fine. Have it your way. But you're mistaken."

"We'll see. . ."

Kathleen was about to argue further, but the blast of cold air blowing through the door silenced her. Josh stomped into the room, carrying a box of tools.

"Here we go," he said breathlessly. "I'll get started repairing the desks."

"That's very thoughtful of you," Kathleen said, making a conscious effort to keep her voice normal. Instead, it had a ring to it that sounded downright fake.

That Mary Bilge had the audacity to chuckle. Kathleen's ire rose. She sent the woman a glare that served only to make her laugh out loud.

"What's so funny, Mary?" Josh asked, shrugging out of his coat. He held his hands over the stove to warm them.

Kathleen sent Mary a silent plea not to further humiliate her.

"I reckon that's my own business," Mary said with a grunt.

Releasing a slow breath, Kathleen gave a grateful smile. Surprise flickered in Mary's eyes, and the hard lines of her face seemed to smooth a bit. She stomped to the door and tossed out her cigar stub, then turned back around. "Well, what are ya standing around gawking for? This here school ain't going to clean itself."

Affection surged through Kathleen. *The old softy.*

Josh brushed his hands together and stood, stretching his back. "That'll have to do for now," he said. He surveyed his handiwork with a sense of satisfaction. He'd repaired four of the damaged desks. The rest were beyond repair and would require rebuilding from the ground up. But he didn't mind. Not if it gave him a few more days to get to know the new teacher.

She smiled at him through a dirt-smudged face. "What a wonderful carpenter you are!"

Pleased embarrassment swept through him. "Thank you. Let's just hope they're sturdy enough."

"I'm sure they are." And to prove her point, she sat in each one and bounced. She grinned up at him. "See?"

Josh laughed out loud. Mary harrumphed. The woman had long since given up trying to help and now sat in the corner, her sharp eyes taking in every move he made. Why she had set herself up as Miss Johnson's watchdog, Josh wasn't sure. But it was apparent the two women held an instant affection for each other.

"Looks to be about suppertime," he mused.

"Oh, I'm sorry I kept you so long, Mr. Truman." Miss Johnson stepped forward and offered her dainty hand. He clasped it gladly, enjoying the smooth warmth of her slender fingers. "Thank you for your assistance. I don't know what I'd have done without you."

Miss Bilge snorted.

Miss Johnson glanced over her shoulder. "I don't know what I'd have done without either of you. You were both sent by God, and I'm truly grateful."

Miss Bilge stood to her full height. "The Almighty wouldn't be sendin' the likes of me to someone such as yourself."

"Of course He would, and He did," the teacher retorted. She grinned and met Miss Bilge across the room. She slipped her arm around the woman's thick shoulders and gave a squeeze. "You're my very first friend here in Coon's Hollow and just like an angel unawares."

For the first time since Josh had known her, Mary Bilge blushed. It wasn't a pretty sight. Rather, she looked like a rabid dog. Her face screwed up, and Josh could have sworn she was about to cry. Instead, she scowled and shook off Miss Johnson's arm. "Angel, my foot." She pinned Josh with her stare. "You takin' her home for supper?"

"Yes, ma'am. If she'll accept the invitation."

"I wouldn't want to impose."

"Mama's expecting you," he assured the girl. "You'd be more than welcome as well, Miss Bilge."

"Thankee kindly, but I got plans. You comin' tomorrow to work some more?"

Josh nodded. "I planned to."

"Fine. I'll be here by nine. Don't come any earlier. Ain't no sense in compromising the girl."

Miss Johnson gasped.

Heat crept up the back of his neck. "Yes, ma'am."

"Well, get on outside and wait in the wagon whilst Miss Johnson cleans up."

Josh couldn't resist a glance at Miss Johnson. Her face

was scarlet, and she didn't quite meet his gaze.

"I'll be waiting," he said softly, trying to put her more at ease. "Take all the time you need."

She nodded, and he exited the schoolroom. He whistled a lively tune as he headed toward the livery to pick up the team. He certainly anticipated the drive home. It would be nice to chat with Miss Johnson without the constant glaring from Miss Bilge.

As the wagon jostled up the pocked lane leading to Josh's house, Kathleen surveyed the white two-story home. A large oak tree stood next to the house, its branches encircling one side of the roof as though they were arms of protection.

"Home, sweet home," Josh said, breaking the silence.

"It's lovely." And it reminded her of her own house back in Rosewood. Loneliness clutched her heart.

Josh reined in the horses and hopped down. He walked to her side of the wagon and reached up to her. "May I?"

She nodded. Her stomach lifted with butterflies when Josh's warm hand closed around hers. He kept a firm grasp as she carefully climbed down. When her feet touched the ground, she looked at him, expecting him to release her hand. But he didn't. Instead, he caught her gaze and smiled. "You have the most beautiful eyes I've ever seen, Miss Johnson."

"I—I don't know what to say."

He placed his finger beneath her chin, the slight pressure encouraging her to return his gaze. "I didn't mean to embarrass you."

They were so close, she could feel his warmth. She'd never stood so close to any man other than family members, and her heart began to race. He smelled of wood smoke and fresh air, and she longed to lean closer. Feelings she didn't understand churned inside her. A wish that he would keep hold of her hand, that he would speak to her in that rich voice, that he would keep looking at her as though he never wanted to look away.

Too soon the moment ended as the door flew open. Kathleen jumped, snatching her hand away.

"Josh! You're finally home!" A little girl hopped off the porch, her brown braids flying behind her as she ran toward them. "Mama was just about to send Pa looking for you."

"Well, we're here. Time got a little away from us."

"I'll say." She turned to look at Kathleen. "I'm Flora Truman. Josh is my brother. You the new teacher?"

Kathleen smiled and held out her hand. "Yes, I am. Pleased to meet you, Flora. I'm Miss Johnson."

"I hope you like it here, Miss Johnson." She heaved a sigh. "Most teachers don't."

"All right," Josh said, taking the little girl by the shoulders and gently turning her toward the house. "Let's go inside."

He offered Kathleen his arm. "Don't let her discourage you. Coon's Hollow isn't so bad once you get used to it."

Unable to resist his boyish grin, she slipped her hand through the crook of his arm and smiled. "I can't help but wonder why your teachers seem to leave. It's not unusual for women to fall in love and marry, thus leaving their positions to be wives, but for someone to just leave for no reason, especially in the middle of the term. . ." She shrugged. "I don't know. It seems a little odd to me."

"It's not unusual for women to fall in love with a local man, eh?" He waggled his eyebrows. "Maybe you'll be a one-term teacher, too."

Kathleen's eyes widened, and she gaped as he opened the door and nudged her inside ahead of him.

Chapter 3

Flopping onto her stomach, Kathleen tried desperately to find a comfortable spot on the straw tick mattress. She grabbed her feather pillow and hugged it into a ball beneath her head. Only the ping of ice balls hitting her window and the occasional *scritch-scratch* coming from the mouse population inside the building penetrated the vast silence.

After a lovely evening at the Trumans', she had enjoyed her ride home with Josh and Flora. But as they approached her teacherage, dread had clenched her stomach. They'd said a hasty good-bye so that Josh could get Flora home and out of the cold. Then the loneliness had set in, and there seemed to be nothing better to do than go to bed.

But sleep never came. Tears rolled down Kathleen's

cheeks, soaking her pillow. She'd never spent the night alone before. Silence permeated the darkness. How she longed for the sound of her brothers' snoring from their respective rooms. The solitude was almost more than she could bear. Mama's words of warning rang in her ears: "Without family around you, Kathleen, you're going to be one miserable young woman. Mark my words."

"Oh, Mama," Kathleen whispered, "you were so right. I should have stayed home where I belong. How will I ever make it here until Christmas break?"

The two months loomed ahead of her as though they were two years. Gentle tears gave way to choking sobs, and finally, just before dawn, only shuddering breaths remained of her sorrowful night.

Despite the gentle light seeping through the cracks in the walls, she was just dozing off when a knock at her door startled her fully awake. Shivering in the cold of the poorly built room, she stepped onto the icy floor and grabbed her dressing gown. She opened the door just a crack.

Miss Bilge stood outside, her arms loaded down with a crate as wide as she was. "Thought you might need some supplies."

Kathleen pulled her wrapper close and peeked at her through the sliver of an opening she'd made when she opened the door. "Good morning, Miss Bilge."

"Well? Ya going to ask me in? Or didn't your ma teach you any manners?"

If it hadn't been so frigid, Kathleen's face would have been hot with embarrassment.

"Yes, ma'am. Come in, please."

Mary shivered and stomped inside. She set the crate on the table and looked about with a scowl Kathleen was beginning to get used to. "Ain't much warmer in here than it is outside. Don't you know how to make a fire?"

"Well, yes, but I haven't had a chance to yet. I just got up."

The woman's gaze swept over Kathleen's attire, and she nodded. "Never been much of a late sleeper myself. Always get up before the chickens."

Defenses raised, Kathleen could just imagine the whole town thinking their new teacher was a stay-a-bed. "I always get up early, too. I just didn't sleep very well last night."

"Why not?"

"I'm just not used to being alone in a new place."

"Well, go on and make yourself decent while I build up the fire," she commanded, waving Kathleen toward the sleeping part of the room. Kathleen ducked behind the curtain. She dressed quickly and made up her bed. By the time she emerged, Mary's fire was already beginning to warm the room, and the table was set with fresh bread, a jar of milk, and a jar of preserves. Mary had pulled out a skillet and stood over slices of ham sizzling on the stove. She turned when Kathleen emerged.

"That's more like it."

Kathleen's curiosity got the better of her, and she peeked inside the box on the table. Flour, sugar, yeast, a crock of butter, fresh eggs, a slab of salt pork, and a pail of lard were packed together. Also, she'd included some apple butter. "Thank you for the provisions, Miss Bilge. Mrs. Truman was kind enough to fill a crate as well, so between the two of you, I'm all fixed up for a while."

"Weren't me, missy. That Mrs. Nelson sent it over."

"The reverend's wife? How kind. I look forward to meeting her on Sunday."

Mary harrumphed. "Not much to look forward to iffen ya ask me."

Picking up on the fact that she'd struck a raw nerve, Kathleen pushed the issue to the back of her mind to discuss with Josh later and broached another topic.

"How long do you suppose it will take before the schoolhouse is ready for the children?"

Mary forked a slice of ham and lifted it to a plate. She shrugged and reached for the second. "Near as I can tell, you oughtta be havin' school by Tuesday or Wednesday of next week. There's holes in the wall that needs to be patched up. Window's got a crack in it and has to be replaced. I reckon someone'll drive into Taneyville and pick one up. Ain't got no ready-made windows 'round here." She glanced at Kathleen. "I reckon young Josh'll be comin' every day to help out."

Kathleen's stomach jumped at the sound of his name. "He's very kind. But I don't want to impose."

"From the looks of it, you'd have to be rude to get rid of him. It's a funny thing. He's never been smitten before, leastways not that I can recall."

"Smitten? Oh, Mary, really. We've only just met."

Mary cracked an egg into the skillet and nodded back at her. "Well, I've known him since he was born, and I say he took a shine to you from the second he laid eyes on ya. And I don't think he's the only one who's sportin' a shine." Setting a plate in front of Kathleen, she cast a sidelong glance.

"I'm sure I don't know what you mean, Mary."

"Ha! I'm sure ya do."

Kathleen was just about to argue further when Mary silenced her with an upraised hand. "No sense denying it to me. I spent the day watchin' ya yesterday. I wouldn't be a bit surprised if he doesn't come courtin' and the two of you end up at the altar before the school term ends. Guess we'll be losin' another teacher after all."

The delicious picture Mary's words conjured up made Kathleen pause and dream—but only for a minute, as the memory of her lonely, sleepless night returned with aching clarity.

Mary's sharp gaze scrutinized her. Kathleen squared her shoulders and forced a firm tone. "You are mistaken. I do not intend to become entangled with anyone in Coon's Hollow. I am going back home in two months. And I'm never leaving home again."

Chapter 4

Sunday morning dawned with warmer temperatures, a brilliant sun, and a return to more fall-like conditions. Kathleen woke much too early from a fitful night's sleep and was ready and waiting a full two hours before Josh arrived to escort her to the worship service. She could feel the stares searing her back as she followed him down the center aisle of the church. The whispers gave way to something akin to a buzzing hive of bees by the time the pair made it to the third row of pews where Josh's family sat.

A man with graying hair and blue eyes, whom Kathleen recognized as Josh's pa, stood and offered his hand. "Nice to have you here, Miss Johnson."

"Thank you." The sight of the large family packed into the pew pinched Kathleen's lonely heart, making her all the more forlorn. Her lip trembled as she smiled at Mrs. Truman. The tiny woman had a kind face, and her returning smile seemed tinged with sympathy. "Are you all settled in, Kathleen?"

"Yes, ma'am. The curtains you gave me last night at dinner spruced the place right up. Thank you."

"I'm so glad." Warmth exuded from her, and Kathleen began to relax. Mrs. Truman turned to the younger boys sitting on the pew. "Alvin, you and Joe move back a row so Josh and Miss Johnson can sit with us."

Kathleen placed her hand on the woman's arm. "Oh, no. I can sit somewhere else. I don't want to put anyone out."

"Nonsense. They don't mind moving." Mrs. Truman waved toward the boys, who were already vacating the pew. "And you two best behave yourselves, or else."

"Yes, Mama," they replied in unison.

Mrs. Truman sat and moved her legs aside so Kathleen and Josh could slide into the seat. Flora sat next to her mother, and Kathleen took the spot next to the little girl. Josh squeezed in on the other side of Kathleen. His warm shoulder pressed against hers, causing her stomach to jump and her pulse to quicken. She pressed her hands together on her lap, reminding herself that Josh could not be the man for her.

Relief washed over her as Reverend Nelson walked to the wooden podium and greeted the congregation.

Kathleen's face grew warm when he singled her out and introduced her as the new teacher. The townsfolk shifted and murmured but didn't seem all that impressed. She had to wonder what was wrong with being the teacher in this town that they couldn't keep one for a full term.

She didn't ponder the question long, however, as the pastor invited a man to the front to lead the congregation in song. Mrs. Nelson's accompaniment on the piano was as beautiful as any music Kathleen had ever heard. The tinny chords seemed to flow outward from her very soul. Indeed, when the preacher's wife played "Blessed Assurance," tears choked Kathleen's throat, and she couldn't sing along.

Reverend Nelson preached a heartfelt message on the subject of contentment, and even with the distraction of Josh's warm shoulder pressed against hers, Kathleen bowed for the closing prayer more moved spiritually than she'd been in a long time.

Though guilt pricked her at her disloyalty to her own pastor, she had to admit Reverend Nelson's gentle delivery and transparent love for God were more inspiring than Rosewood's eighty-four-year-old pulpit-pounding preacher, Obadiah Strong.

After the benediction and subsequent dismissal, Mr. Truman turned to Kathleen. "I hope you'll come to the farm for Sunday dinner, Miss Johnson. My sister, Estelle, and the pastor will be joining us as well."

Relief washed over her. Her greatest dread had been what she would do with herself for an entire Sunday afternoon alone. She felt a gentle squeeze on her elbow and turned to meet Josh's gaze. He smiled. "Please join us. It would be my honor to escort you home this evening."

"Well, of course she's coming." Mrs. Nelson seemed to have appeared out of nowhere. "If we hadn't accepted Susan's invitation to dinner, I would have insisted the new teacher come have dinner with us. So, Miss Johnson," she said firmly but with a smile, "you must say yes."

"Then yes it is. And thank you for your kind invitation, Mr. and Mrs. Truman." She turned to the preacher's wife and grinned. "And Mrs. Nelson."

As had been the case the previous two nights, dinner at the Truman farm proved to be a noisy, fun affair. Only Josh's younger brother Alvin ate in silence while the rest of the family spoke above one another, laughing and reaching until Kathleen couldn't help but feel right at home.

When the last bite had been eaten, Flora hopped up and tugged at Kathleen's sleeve. "Eliza had puppies.

They're so cute. Do you want to see them, Miss Johnson?"

"I suppose so, if it's all right with your ma and pa."

"Not so fast, little girl," Mr. Truman spoke up, placing a restraining hand on the child's arm. "First you have to help your ma clean up."

"I'll help, too," Kathleen offered, seeing the little girl's expression plummet. "Then maybe we can go see the puppies afterward."

Mrs. Truman stood and picked up the empty platter that had been laden with fluffy biscuits an hour earlier. "You'll do nothing of the kind," she said firmly. "As a guest in this house, you are not allowed to lift a finger to help. Josh, please escort Kathleen to the barn and show her the new puppies. Flora, honey, grab a towel and get ready to dry the dishes."

Flora scowled but looked down quickly before her mother noticed. "Yes, ma'am," she mumbled.

Kathleen's heart went out to her, and when Flora ventured a glance, she couldn't resist a wink at the child. Flora's expression brightened considerably, and she scurried off toward the kitchen.

Josh stood. "Shall we go and see the wiggly bunch of mongrels in the barn?"

Mindful of the vast interest coming from the family members still seated around the table, Kathleen felt her cheeks warm. "You don't really have to show me the puppies," she said.

His smile fled. "You don't want to see them? Or you'd prefer to wait for Flora?"

Was it her imagination, or did he seem deflated?

"Oh, no. I'd love to see them."

"With Flora?"

"Or you. I just didn't want you to feel obligated."

"It would be my pleasure to escort you to see the new puppies, Miss Johnson."

His adolescent brother, Joe, snickered. Josh's face tinged with pink, then deepened a shade when even tight-lipped Alvin joined the laughter. Soon, even the pastor couldn't hold back a smile.

Mr. Truman stood and slapped Josh on the back. "If you two don't head on out to the barn, those pups are bound to be weaned and having pups of their own by the time you finally get around to it."

"Yes, sir." His brown eyes seemed to entreat her to hurry and get him out of the humiliating situation.

With a nod, she rose and placed her napkin on the table. "Please excuse me," she murmured to the family without making eye contact with any of them.

She could feel Josh's relief match her own when they were outside, away from the amusement-filled room.

"Your family is quite nice," she said, if for no other reason than to break the heavy silence.

"Thanks. Sometimes they're a bit much. I'm sorry if they made you uncomfortable."

Kathleen laughed. "Being the only girl in a house with four brothers, I'm used to teasing. As a matter of fact, I miss it. So in a way, your family's ribbing helped ease my homesickness a bit."

Josh reached out to lift the latch on the barn door. "Are you very homesick? You've only been here two nights."

"I've never been away from home before."

He nodded, stepping aside so that she could precede him into the barn. "I suppose I can understand that. Are you sorry you didn't take one look at the school and high-tail it home like Mary suggested? Please don't say you are. I'll be completely crushed if you do."

He grinned, and Kathleen nearly melted into a puddle. She chuckled at his crooked smile but answered honestly. "When I'm around people, I know I made the right decision. But it's difficult for me to be alone. The funny thing is that growing up I always longed for privacy. I often take a book and go down by the little creek that runs through our property and just sit for hours and hours reading and being alone with my thoughts. But now the solitude is almost painful."

As soon as the last sentence left her lips, Kathleen regretted it. She hadn't meant to be so transparent, but Josh's obvious concern combined with her need for conversation had brought the admission tumbling out. Before he could answer, she wandered away from his side and followed the sound of whimpering until she found a scruffy black-and-white mama dog surrounded by wiggling pups.

Approaching cautiously, Kathleen expected the dog to growl. Instead, the animal gave a welcoming whine. Kneeling on the hay, Kathleen reached out and stroked the mama dog's head while the blind puppies whined and nuzzled, trying to find a place to nurse.

"I don't believe it. Only Flora's been able to get anywhere near that dog since she had those pups day before yesterday."

"Well, she knows a friendly soul when she sees one. Don't you, sweet girl?" she crooned. "May I hold one of your babies?" Gingerly, she eased her hand under one of the milk-rounded bellies and lifted a shiny black pup. It trembled until she snuggled it close, speaking in soft, reassuring tones. "Oh, you're just so precious."

Kathleen could feel Josh watching her. She glanced up. Tenderness shone from those wonderful eyes, and his full mouth curved into a smile. "Sort of makes a fellow wish he was a puppy," he said, his voice husky and barely above a whisper.

She blinked. "I beg your pardon?"

"The way you're holding the puppy makes me wonder what it would be like to have your arms around me."

A gasp escaped her lips, and she set the dog down, then scrambled to her feet. Tossing out a look of utter disdain, she stomped past him toward the door.

"Wait, Miss Johnson." He caught up to her and took her firmly but gently by the arm, turning her to face him. "Kathleen, I'm sorry I offended you."

"I do not know what sort of woman you think I am, sir." Kathleen's lip trembled as it always did when she was angry.

"I think you're a fine young lady. And I can't help but admire you. Is that so wrong?"

"In so much that you are imagining my—my arms about you, it is quite wrong." Her voice cracked under the embarrassment. Her mind conjured the lecherous smile from the man at the train station, and her ire rose even higher. "I have never met such ill-mannered young men before in my life. And that's no affront to your ma's raising of you, either. I'm sure she did her best."

Rather than apologizing, Josh planted his feet, releasing her arm. A muscle twitched in his square jaw. "I don't know what sort of men court you back home, but if they don't admit to wondering what it would be like to hold you in their arms, they're just not being truthful."

"Wondering it and saying it are two different things, *Mister* Truman."

"Well, saying it and *doing* it are two different things as well."

He took a daring step closer. Kathleen's pulse sped up like a runaway train. Her thoughts jumbled together. Was he going to try to kiss her? Surely she couldn't allow such a thing. She moistened her lips. Josh's hand slid around her waist, and he pulled her close. A warm woozy feeling enveloped her, rendering her unable to think straight. She barely registered his head descending. Oh, Ma would be mortified. But how could Kathleen resist?

She was just about to close her eyes and surrender to her first kiss when the creaking of the barn door jolted her back to her senses. She leaped from his embrace as Flora skipped into the barn.

"Did you see the puppies? Aren't they adorable? Ma said I can keep only one. But I can't decide which one I like best. Which one do you like best, Miss Johnson?"

"I, um, I don't really know. I only held one." She tried to concentrate on the little girl's words, but Josh's nearness and the memory of what had almost occurred between them had her so rattled, she barely remembered her own name.

"Which?" Flora pressed.

"Um, a black one, I think."

"Oh, I like the black ones. There are two of those."

"Are there?" Why couldn't she take her gaze from Josh's? There was no triumph in his eyes, as one might expect from a young man who knew he'd almost been successful in his quest to steal a kiss. Rather, the look in his eyes nearly stole her breath away. His eyes spoke his respect for her, and only a quick glance to her lips and back to her eyes betrayed his regret that the kiss had been interrupted before it began.

Kathleen felt her own regrets at the moment. Later, however, after Josh, accompanied by Flora and Joe, had escorted her home and she sat alone drinking a cup of tea, she remembered Ma's edict. The Lord knew quite well where Kathleen lived. He was quite capable of sending the right young man to Rosewood. She didn't need to go off looking elsewhere.

Shame infused her. The guilty knowledge that she'd been on the verge of actually allowing a kiss made her squirm. She and her friends had a word for girls who teased the boys: *fast.* The only thing was that it didn't feel like she was being forward. It felt like a cozy fire on a cold day. Like the warm promise of spring as green grass pushed through thawed earth, the budding flowers after a dreary, colorless winter. That's what it had felt like when Josh held her close.

Kathleen shook herself from her thoughts. She had no intention of allowing herself to become infatuated with a boy living outside of Rosewood. How could she bear to be separated from her family permanently when two days away from them seemed like an eternity? She chewed her lip as she pondered the thought. Perhaps Josh would move to Rosewood. He could join Pa and the brothers at the livery.

Kathleen laughed into the empty room. She'd known him for two measly days, and already she was planning his future for him.

That night, as she crawled into bed, she resolved to banish all romantic thoughts of Josh Truman. She had a job to do, and she would do it well. When her term was up, she'd return home and never, ever leave Rosewood again. If only she could convince herself of that fact. Instead, her traitorous brain insisted on replaying the scene in the barn over and over until finally she drifted into a dreamless sleep.

Chapter 5

Kathleen rubbed her arms vigorously, trying to generate heat in the cold schoolroom while she waited for the newly built fire to warm the chill in the morning air. She glanced about with a satisfied nod.

It had taken her, Josh, and Mary Bilge the better part of a week—with the exception of the Lord's Day—to make the school presentable. Now the odor of fresh paint hung in the room, and the walls shone white without a smudge. The single window sparkled, and not a speck of dust could be seen on the desks or floor. And she'd already swept up this morning's traces of mouse droppings.

Kathleen knew pride was sinful, but as she surveyed their handiwork, she couldn't hold back a smile. They had taken a room filled with broken desks and scattered materials from messy to ready in such a short time. She glanced at the watch pinned to her dress and felt her heart pick up a few beats. The children would be arriving soon. Her palms dampened at the thought.

Despite her nervousness, she hoped to discover the reason Coon's Hollow couldn't seem to keep a teacher for more than half a term. From her admittedly limited experience, the townsfolk didn't seem overly friendly, but neither were they rude—with the exception of the man in the train station upon her arrival. So she had to wonder why there was such a turnover of teachers that the seedier citizens had a running pool every time a new teacher arrived.

A wide yawn stretched her mouth. At least the nervousness served to keep her from dozing off. Sleep still eluded her at night. She had taken to heeding David's psalms. *In the night his song shall be with me, and my prayer unto the God of my life.*

What else was there to do but sing and pray to God when one was completely alone and wrestling insomnia? Sleeplessness was doing wonders for her spiritual life. Unfortunately, her physical body was running down.

Twenty minutes before school was set to begin, the door opened. Kathleen gave a startled glance up. Mary stomped in, her cigar hanging from her lips.

Kathleen scowled. "The cigar, Mary."

"What about it?"

"The children will soon begin arriving. I would rather they not be subjected to the sight of anyone smoking. It sends the wrong signal."

"Smoke signals? Ain't been no Injuns 'round these parts for quite some time. Leastways, none that'd be inclined to send up a signal." Mary cackled at her own joke.

Holding back a smile so as not to encourage her, Kathleen shook her head.

With a sigh, Mary straightened up. "Oh, okay. What sorta signal?"

Kathleen hesitated. She was loath to offend the woman, but neither could she take a chance on one of the children walking in to find Mary smoking in the school. She chose her words carefully. "I'm sure you understand that I can't allow it to appear as though I condone the practice. To children that would send a message that I believe it's all right for them to do the same. I am in charge of this classroom of students, and I must be morally upright."

"Well, la-de-da." Mary snorted but tossed her cigar out the door, then let it bang shut.

Somewhat surprised by the easy compliance, Kathleen gave her a thankful smile. "What can I do for you this morning, Mary?"

"Thought I'd come see how your first day's going."

A smile tipped Kathleen's lips. "Hmm, let me see. I got up, made my bed, and dressed. I ate a little bread for breakfast and wiped off my table. Then I came in here to build the fire. And that's about it so far."

Mary smirked, obviously appreciating Kathleen's humor. "Guess it is a bit early. I best get me on to the preacher's house. That missus of his wants me to scrub down the walls today." She shook her head in disgust. "I think she just does it to see me workin' hard. Like she's lording it over me just 'cause the reverend married her 'stead of me. Ya want to know why he picked her?"

"Why?"

" 'Cause I'm too much woman for him, that's why." She gave a decisive nod. "I just don't know what to say about a man that settles for a woman like that." With a heavy sigh, she clomped toward the door. "I best get on over there before she takes it as a reason to let me go. If they didn't pay so good. . ."

Kathleen stared in bewildered silence. Josh had told her that Mary worked for the preacher and his wife. And that the woman had once locked Mrs. Nelson in the cellar, but no one could prove it, and Mary wasn't confessing.

When she reached the door, Mary turned. "Now don't worry about anything today. If them rapscallions get out of hand, you give 'em a good smack. I'll be around at noon to check on ya and see how things are going."

Affection surged through Kathleen. Now she understood what had prompted Mary to stop by. She knew Kathleen would be a bundle of nerves at the anticipation of the children's arrival. "Thank you for the suggestion. Let's hope it doesn't come to anything more forceful than a stern word or at worst a few minutes in the corner."

"Harrumph. That last teacher didn't believe in corporal punishment, either. And look where she is now. Sometimes a good whack on the behind is the only thing a child understands. Spare the rod and spoil the child. And all that Bible stuff."

The word *Bible* reminded Kathleen of Mary's absence from church on Sunday. Though today was Wednesday, she'd forgotten to ask the woman about it. "Were you feeling poorly on Sunday, Mary?"

"Poorly? Me? No, ma'am, I'm as fit as a fiddle." She narrowed her bushy brows. "Why'd ya ask?"

"I missed you in church."

To Kathleen's surprise, Mary flushed, and pleasure lit the slightly yellowish countenance. "Go on, now. You didn't miss me."

"No, I really did. I don't have many friends in town, and I was looking for a familiar face."

"Well, I don't go in for religion much. I gave it a try about a year ago. But that was before. . ."

Before the preacher got married. Though Kathleen was aware of the woman's crush on the preacher, she would no more have humiliated Mary by letting her know than she would have admitted her own crush on the preacher's nephew-in-law Josh.

"It's a shame you stopped going. But it's never too late to return to the house of God."

"So you really missed me, did ya?"

"Yes."

"I might show up on Sunday. If I don't got nothin' better to do."

"That would be wonderful. I'll save you a seat."

A rare smile split the woman's face, showing a surprisingly healthy set of teeth. "You'd do that? Sit next to me and all?"

"Why, Mary, you have a beautiful smile. You should display it more often. And yes, I would be honored to sit beside you during the service."

Mary turned four shades of red, cleared her throat, and frowned. She slapped her man's hat onto her head. "Well, don't get your heart set on it. I said maybe." Without giving Kathleen another chance to speak, she opened the door and paused. "You look out for that Myles Carpenter, now. We think he's harmless enough. But you just never can tell with crazy people."

Before Kathleen could ask what she meant, Mary slipped through the door, slamming it shut behind her.

Kathleen didn't have much time to ponder Mary's warning, as two minutes later the first of a steady stream of students arrived. Boys and girls ranging in age from five to fifteen—a total of twenty-four in all.

Her legs trembled a bit as she called the school to order and the children took their seats, silently watching her. . .waiting for her to speak. She spotted Flora sitting in the second row of desks. Her glossy brown braids were tied with two blue ribbons that matched her eyes. Kathleen smiled, amazed at the difference a friendly face could make in such a nerve-racking situation.

Clearing her throat, she looked from left to right, including each child with her smile. "Good morning."

A scattered mumbling of "good mornings" came in reply. Not a very friendly group. But she'd warm them up in no time. She hoped.

"Let's begin the day by saying the Lord's Prayer. Please stand and remain next to your desks."

The sound of chairs scraping the floor followed as the children rose. Kathleen closed her eyes and took a deep breath as she started the prayer. When they'd finished with "for thine is the kingdom and the power and the glory forever, amen," she opened her eyes, ready to start her first day as a teacher.

By noon, she wished she'd gone back to Rosewood while the getting was good. Now it was too late, despite the unresponsive, disinterested children who barely knew the material. To make matters worse, they were unruly. Jonah Barker had yanked on Flora's braid hard, eliciting a howl from the girl and a retaliatory smack in the face. Kathleen had been forced to stand them both in the corner for thirty minutes. Snickers from the students during arithmetic had confused her until she realized Jonah was making faces at her. She'd commanded him to stand in the back corner where she could keep an eye on him after that.

Now she sat alone eating her lunch of leftover ham between two thick slices of bread. She finished her sandwich all too quickly and stuffed her napkin inside the pail, then glanced at her watch. The children were allowed a full hour for lunch; forty-five minutes remained. She ventured to the window and smiled at the sight of her students playing baseball in the schoolyard.

Wandering back to her seat, she yawned. Her eyes felt gritty from lack of sleep. The desktop looked so inviting that she folded her arms over the desk and rested her head. What could it hurt for just a few minutes? She closed her eyes and felt powerless as she slowly drifted to sleep.

Josh frowned as he heard the sound of children's laughter. He knew it was half past two because he'd just checked his watch a moment earlier. Why were the children outside?

He pulled into the schoolyard. Flora gave him an uncertain smile. He motioned her over.

"Hi, Josh. How come you're in town? It isn't time to pick me up yet, is it?"

"No. Ma sent me for some sugar at the dry goods store. Why are you outside playing instead of inside learning?"

Flora shrugged. "Miss Johnson never rang the bell after lunch, so David Kirk said we should just keep playing until she came out. Only she never did. I looked inside a little while ago, and her head is down on top of her desk. Sarah Thomas said she might be dead. I'm too scared to go find out." Flora's blue eyes implored him. "You don't think she's dead, do you?"

"Of course not, honey." Concern knotted his stomach. He wrapped the reins around the brake and hopped down from the wagon seat. "You stay outside while I go check on her, okay?"

Flora nodded. Josh recognized the look of worry in her eyes. He patted her shoulder. "Don't worry, sugar. I'm sure Miss Johnson is just fine."

He reached the door and slowly stepped inside. As Flora had said, Kathleen was at her desk with her head resting on her arms. With no attempt to keep his boots from making noise on the wood floor, he clomped up the aisle. His heart nearly stopped until he saw the rise and fall of her shoulders. Then it nearly melted. Tenderness such as he'd never before experienced washed over him. He reached out and caressed her silken cheek with the back of his hand. Still she didn't budge.

"Kathleen," he said, keeping his voice soft so as not to startle her. He squatted beside her. "Kathleen, honey, wake up."

With slow movements, she shifted, sighed, and nestled back into sleep.

Josh smiled and gave her shoulder a gentle shake. "Kathleen."

She moaned and shifted. Then her eyes became slits. In a beat, they opened fully. She gasped and sat up. "Josh!"

"Good morning, sleepyhead."

"Morning? What time is it?" Without waiting for an answer, she grabbed at her brooch watch. "Oh no! The children. Lunch was over an hour and a half ago. Where are they?"

"They're still outside playing baseball. They thought you were dead."

First her eyes widened in horror, but as she observed his laughter, her own lips curved upward. She lifted her eyebrow. "Baseball, huh? My untimely demise must not have weighed too heavily on their little minds."

He chuckled. "Flora wanted to check on you, but she was too scared to take the chance, just in case you really were dead. You know how young 'uns are."

With a moan, she pressed the heels of her hands against her forehead. "How could I have fallen asleep like that? The school board will be sure to send me packing now."

"I don't think you have to worry about that. It's not as though they'll likely get yet another replacement this term."

A frown puckered her brow, adding to the lines still imprinted from her dress sleeves. "Josh, can I ask you something?"

When she gave him that beguiling, innocently confused look from beautiful blue eyes, she could ask him anything. He swallowed hard and tried to focus. "Sure."

"Why does Coon's Hollow have such a hard time keeping teachers? Pa said no teacher has ever stayed for a second term. And I know I'm taking over for the last one."

Josh stood and shrugged. "I guess a town like this isn't exactly too enticing for a young woman. Plus. . ." He hesitated.

"What?"

"Well, I take it Myles Carpenter didn't show up today?"

"Mary Bilge mentioned him as well, but I don't recall a child by that name."

"Myles isn't a child, except in his mind. He's about seventy."

"Then why would you ask if he showed up at school?"

"Sometimes he gets a little confused and thinks he's the teacher."

At her look of alarm, he hurried on. "He's a little strange but harmless. Unfortunately, he doesn't seem to value cleanliness, so he doesn't look or smell too great."

She wrinkled her nose and shook her head. "That's a shame, but what does it have to do with Coon's Hollow's inability to keep a teacher?"

He took a breath. "Apparently, Myles was once a schoolmaster. Then the War Between the States started, and he left to fight. When he came back, he wasn't the same. His wife welcomed him home, but they never had children. She died about ten years ago. The old-timers say Myles lost what was left of his mind when she passed on."

Pity clouded Kathleen's eyes. "How sad."

"Yes, and most of the teachers feel that same compassion until he orders them from his classroom three or four times." Josh smiled. "The board goes to him, and he promises to behave, but he always ends up back at the school. I've never thought him to be crazy, to be honest. Personally, I think he drinks too much."

"Oh, my. Does he frighten the children?"

"Naw. They're used to him."

"Well, I'll be on the lookout. Thank you for giving me advance warning."

"I suppose I should have told you sooner. But I was afraid you might not stay."

A smile curved her full lips. "I might not have."

He gazed speechless into her eyes, and it was all he could do not to finish the kiss he'd almost started a few days ago in the barn. Obviously, she realized his train of thought, because her eyes grew wide, and she shifted back. "Josh," she said, her voice faltering. "You need to know something."

"Yes?" He couldn't concentrate on anything when she looked at him that way.

"I'm not. . .free to become attached to anyone." Her

eyelashes fluttered downward as she studied her hands in her lap.

Feeling like a bull had kicked him right in the gut, Josh winced. "I see. You're already spoken for by someone in your hometown?"

She glanced up quickly. "Oh no. Nothing like that."

Relief shattered the sick feeling of defeat. "Then you're free to be courted properly. You don't have to worry. I can restrain myself as long as we don't spend too much time alone. I won't try to steal any more kisses."

Her face turned several shades of pink. "It's. . .I mean I am free in that I'm not being courted by anyone." She gathered a long breath. "What I meant to say is that I cannot allow myself to become attached to a man who lives so far away from my family. I don't want to live apart from them."

That sick feeling stole over him again as he realized she was saying he had no chance. "I see."

"Do you?" Her beautiful blue eyes implored him to understand.

He was trying. Smiling, he pressed her hand. "Then we'll be good friends? Deal?"

Hesitation shone across her features, and Josh swallowed hard and hurried to add, "You don't want to go to the dance next month all by yourself."

"Dance?"

"Fall dance. We usually hold it earlier in October, but with the teacher leaving so suddenly and all, no one had the heart. It'll be the second Saturday of November."

"I see. Maybe I'll just stay home."

"A girl like you doesn't stay home from dances. Besides, it's held in the schoolhouse." He grinned.

Her lips twitched in amusement. "Maybe I'll go alone."

Josh knew they were playing a game, and he played along. "All right. But without an escort, all the fellows will buzz around and try to court you. You'll be doing an awful lot of explaining about how you're not to court anyone not from Rosewood."

She narrowed her gaze. "Are you teasing me or making fun?"

Tenderly, he knelt beside her and took her hand and pressed it to his heart. "I promise you, I will never make fun of you."

Tears sprang to her eyes, making them look like two clear pools. It was all Josh could do not to move in for a kiss. But she'd made her position clear. He had no intention of letting her go if there was any way to change her mind. But he'd let her get to know him. If he had to be her protector, her friend, until she realized he was the man for her, then so be it. He'd finally found the woman of his dreams, and he'd be a no-good disappointment to generations of Truman men if he didn't try his best to win her love.

Flora took that moment to burst into the schoolroom. "Josh! Come quick! Jonah's beating up Andrew Coon. We can't get them to stop."

Chapter 6

Kathleen fought tears as a paper wad zinged past her ear and smacked the wall behind her. She surveyed the unruly room—proof of her utter failure as a teacher—then allowed her gaze to settle on Flora. The girl stared back, her wide blue eyes clearly asking her why she was putting up with such shameful conduct from the boys.

The answer was that they were big. At fifteen, Andrew Coon was the size of a grown man. She was clearly at a disadvantage, and he knew it. Therefore, ever since the first humiliating day when she'd fallen asleep—had that really only been two weeks ago?—Andrew had essentially run the class. No one was learning, and she could barely hear herself think above the chatter and shouting.

A glance at her clock revealed a depressing one-thirty.

Too early to dismiss.

Oh, Lord. What am I going to do?

Outside, the wind howled, shaking the place, and she found herself almost wishing for a blizzard to close the school down for a few days.

"Ow, Miss Johnson, help!"

The sound of Melissa Sharpton's pain-filled cry pulled Kathleen from her fog, and she leaped to her feet. "What is it, Melissa?"

Tears pooled in the eight-year-old's eyes.

Behind her, Andrew cleared his throat. . .loudly.

"Well, Melissa?" Kathleen asked.

"N—nothing."

Kathleen turned to Andrew. Triumph shone in his eyes. Indignation lit a fire inside Kathleen. Clearly the bully was terrorizing the smaller children.

"Andrew, I would like for you to stand in the corner."

"What for, teacher? I didn't do nothin'."

He had a point—she hadn't absolutely caught him. Still, she couldn't back down now. Not if she were ever to have a prayer of regaining control of her class. She planted one hand on her hip and pointed with the other. "In the corner. Now!"

The room became deathly silent. Andrew sneered. "I ain't doin' it."

Out-and-out defiance. Exactly what she'd been afraid of and the very reason she'd failed to confront Andrew thus far. Now what was she supposed to do? "You will obey me, or you will not return to my classroom. Is that clear?"

"Ain't nothin' you can do about it. I'm a Coon."

"I don't care if you're a squirrel. You'll do as I say."

The children snickered at her joke.

Andrew's face deepened to a dark red. "Shut up!" he bellowed. The room fell silent once more.

A gust of wind jolted them from the intensity of the moment. All eyes turned toward the open door. Kathleen gasped as a man—who could only be Myles Carpenter—walked regally into the room. Though layered in filth and crowned with a thick head of uncombed gray hair, Mr. Carpenter owned the room from the moment he appeared.

"What can I do for you, sir?" Kathleen walked cautiously toward him.

"What can you do for me, young lady? You can control your students, that's what."

At least for the moment, he recognized that *she* was the teacher.

"What was that hollering I heard coming from in here?"

What did she have to lose? If she was going to be

criticized by the town crazy man, how long was she going to have her job anyway?

She gathered a deep sigh. "I'm afraid that was Andrew Coon. He is disobedient, rude, and refuses to be disciplined."

The man's gaze narrowed. Then he turned to the classroom. "Which one of you, may I ask, is Andrew Coon?"

Every set of eyes in the room turned to stare at the culprit, but Andrew averted his gaze. Clearly his pride in his name had all but vanished.

But Mr. Carpenter got the hint. His odor trailed behind him as he sauntered across the room, his back straight as an English butler's.

Kathleen gathered the sides of her skirt into the balls of her fists to keep from pinching her nose.

"Stand up, young man," Mr. Carpenter ordered.

With a nervous laugh, Andrew turned his head and stared at the window as though he hadn't heard the man speak. In a flash, Myles's hand shot out. He grabbed Andrew by the scruff of his collar and lifted him to a standing position, knocking his chair back in the process.

"Hey! Turn me loose, old man! Wait 'til I tell my pa."

Despite Andrew's size, Mr. Carpenter had a good three inches of height on him. His strength seemed amazing as Andrew's attempts to free himself failed. "You have a deplorable lack of manners, boy." Keeping a firm grasp on Andrew's collar, Mr. Carpenter turned to Kathleen. "What would you have me do with the lad, miss?"

Kathleen blinked and fought to regain her voice. "I. . .in the corner, please."

"There are four of them; please specify."

Remembering the ridicule from Jonah the first day of school, she knew better than to stand Andrew in the corner behind her desk. She pointed to the back of the room. "Over there."

Mr. Carpenter nodded his filthy head, and Kathleen cringed at the layers of dirt encrusted on his neck. "Good choice," he said.

Laughter buzzed about the room as Myles walked Andrew on tiptoes to the corner. Kathleen looked about and shook her head for them to hush. They complied. Apparently no one wanted to be Mr. Carpenter's next target.

When he reached the corner of choice, Mr. Carpenter simply let Andrew go. "And stay there until your teacher says you may return to your seat. Is that clear?"

Obviously startled into submission, Andrew nodded without turning around. But Mr. Carpenter wasn't finished. "When school is dismissed, you will stay afterward and clean up the mess. It is disgraceful."

Perhaps his last comment was a bit like the pot calling the kettle black; still, Kathleen couldn't help but be grateful to the gentleman.

She expelled a pent-up breath, then wished she hadn't as she was forced to breathe in at the same time Mr. Carpenter returned to confront her. Fighting to contain her nausea, she offered a wobbly smile.

Her cheeks flooded with warmth at his look of utter contempt.

"You must show them who is in charge or you are wasting their time."

Their time?

Though he dwarfed her, she gathered herself to her full height, raised her chin, and looked him in the eye. "Thank you for your help, Mr. Carpenter. I'm sure I can take it from here."

His disparaging look told her more than she cared to know about his opinion of whether she could handle the situation. Nevertheless, he scowled and walked to the door, his shoulders squared. Such a show of dignity touched Kathleen's heart.

He turned when he reached the door. Though his face was caked with grime, his hazel eyes pierced her. "These children have precious few years to learn anything at all before their Neanderthal fathers stick them in the cornfields and squash the greater portion of all that wonderful knowledge from their heads. You must pack as much into their brains as possible, so that perchance they will retain what is most relevant."

He slipped through the door and was gone as quickly as he'd come.

Dread gnawed Kathleen's gut as she glanced toward the corner. At the very least, she expected Andrew to lean against the wall. But to her delight, he stayed put. Perhaps he was afraid Mr. Carpenter was watching from a window somewhere. Or perhaps the stench had rattled his brain. Whatever the case, after thirty minutes, she took pity and quietly suggested he return to his seat. He obeyed, sitting while the rest of the children took their turn at reciting their spelling words.

It was ten minutes after three before Kathleen realized they were over the time for school to be let out. "School is dismissed," she announced. In subdued silence, the children rose, gathered their belongings, and left in an orderly fashion.

She leaned her elbows on her desk, closed her eyes, and rested her forehead in the heels of her hands. Taking a few deep breaths, she willed herself to relax. When the door opened again a minute later, she looked up and gasped. Andrew stood, hands stuffed into his pockets.

She swallowed hard. Was he planning his revenge? Whatever the case, she couldn't show her fear. "Did you forget something, Andrew?"

"Yes." He sauntered up the aisle. He hesitated then scowled. "That crazy ol' Myles told me to clean the room after school."

She'd completely forgotten!

"Thank you for coming back, Andrew. The place is quite a mess."

"Yeah."

"How about if we clean it up together?"

He shrugged but remained silent as they spent the next fifteen minutes removing wads of paper, chalk, pencils, and even crusts of bread from the floor.

"I think that about does it," Kathleen announced.

"Fine. I'm leavin' then."

"All right. And Andrew?"

"Yeah."

"You know we're putting on a Christmas program the week before school gets out."

"What of it?"

"I was hoping you'd consider playing Joseph."

Interest sparked in his eyes, and Kathleen proceeded before she lost her nerve.

"Yes, Rebecca Dunn has already agreed to play Mary."

His face turned three shades of red. "Rebecca?"

A bit of guilt nipped her insides like a troublesome pup. She'd caught Andrew staring at an oblivious Rebecca more than once. She figured he might have a chance if he'd simmer down.

"Yes. I thought the two of you would make a handsome Mary and Joseph. What do you say?"

He kicked at the floor with his boot and shrugged. "Ain't got nothing better to do."

"I take it that's a yes?"

A sigh lifted his chest. "I guess."

"Wonderful. We start rehearsal Monday after school. Please tell your pa to come speak to me if he has any problems with you remaining after class."

"He ain't gonna care." He slipped through the door before Kathleen could press further.

Kathleen stared at the closed door for a few seconds. After one last look at her tidy schoolroom, she adjourned to her quarters for another lonely evening.

"Then he stayed in the corner until Miss Johnson told him he could sit down."

Josh listened to Flora's recounting of her afternoon with a combination of concern and amusement.

"And he didn't order her from her classroom?" Ma asked, setting a platter of ham on the table.

"No, ma'am. He didn't seem all that crazy to me. Just stank real bad."

"Flora! Don't be rude."

"Sorry, Ma. But he did. Bad." She grinned at Josh. "Miss Johnson looked like she might faint. Everyone said so."

Ma cleared her throat, a clear sign that Josh was not to encourage the child.

"Paul, perhaps we should speak to Frank about this. After all, he is the preacher. If anyone should talk to Myles, it should be him."

"How do you figure? Myles hasn't darkened the doorstep of our church in longer than I can remember— not since Frank asked him to kindly take a bath." He winked at Flora. "So that the ladies didn't faint at the smell of him."

Flora giggled, and Ma frowned at them both.

"I suppose you're right about Frank. All the same, someone should talk to him about not interrupting Miss Johnson's class. After all, the young woman is doing us a kindness by taking over at the last minute. How many more teachers are we going to let that man run off?"

"Miss Johnson didn't seem to mind him too much."

Joe spoke with a mouthful of potatoes.

"Mercy, Joe," Ma admonished. "Swallow first."

He swallowed hard, then washed down the bite with a gulp of milk. He wiped his mouth with the back of his hand, forked another bite, and held it in front of his mouth. "Miss Johnson was a lot nicer to him than the other teachers ever were." He shoveled the bite inside.

Josh listened to this news with tenderness. Her kindness was only one reason he was falling for Kathleen Johnson.

Still, Ma didn't seem convinced. "Well, the girl's obviously been raised with better manners than some, but that doesn't mean she'll put up with constant interruptions, especially if he gets confused. Someone had better give him a good talking to before he runs her off like all the others." She gave Pa a pointed look, but Josh judged from Pa's scowl that he had no intention of butting into the situation.

Her gaze shifted to Josh.

He nodded. He only had a few weeks to prove to the girl of his dreams that he was the man for her, even if he did live fifty miles away from her family. There was no way he would let an outside influence like a crazy former schoolmaster send her running home even one day earlier than absolutely necessary.

Chapter 7

Kathleen shot straight up, unsure why she'd awakened so suddenly. Outside, the wind howled and shook the thin boards. The fire had died down, and the air inside the room bit through her, chilling her to the bone. She pulled the quilt up to her neck and shivered in an attempt to warm herself. Finally, she pushed the covers aside and tiptoed across the icy floor to the stove.

Moments later, wood crackled as the glowing coals caught. Another gust of wind shook the little room.

She shuddered. The clock on a shelf over the stove clearly showed four o'clock. Too early to get up. Yawning, she headed back to her bed.

Thump, thump.

Footsteps? Cold fear swept through Kathleen as the

sound in the schoolroom came closer. She eyed the door that separated the two rooms and was suddenly aware of the absence of a lock. She spun around, searching for anything with which to defend herself. Hesitating only a second, she snatched up a large kitchen knife and inched toward the door.

Crash!

Kathleen jumped, her heart nearly beating from her chest. Clutching the knife firmly with both hands, she listened for more sounds. Anything that might mean someone was about to burst through her door. Numbness crept into her feet as she remained barefoot on the icy floor.

Muscles knotted, stomach tight, she waited, and waited. . .and waited until, finally, the fire died again, and she was forced to hang on to the knife with one hand and add wood to the stove with the other. Muted light slowly expelled the darkness from the room, and when Kathleen dared to take her gaze from the door, she noted the clock read seven-thirty.

The children would be arriving for school in less than an hour. How could she cower in her room and allow any one of them to step into a possibly dangerous situation?

Lord, give me courage.

Reaching out with trembling fingers, she grabbed the

latch, gathered a deep breath, and flung open the door. A split second seemed like an eternity as she waited for her attacker to strike. When all remained calm, she took a cautious step across the doorway.

A body lay atop the remains of one of the newly repaired desks. She couldn't make out a face, but the stench was unmistakable. Her heart beat a rain dance within her chest as she approached. She grimaced at the thought of having to touch his filthy chest to ascertain whether or not he was breathing. He moaned, and she jumped back.

Relief like a fresh summer breeze washed over her, and her wobbly legs refused to hold her another second. She made it to the last desk and sank into the seat, dropping the knife to the ground.

The clatter woke her intruder.

"What on earth is that racket?"

Kathleen blinked as he sat up, brushing away the splintered wood.

He was asking *her* about racket?

"Well? Speak up!"

"I—I dropped my knife."

"Why, pray tell, do you have a weapon inside the school? You are not fit to teach these children. I knew that from the first moment I saw you."

Tears pricked her eyes, and her throat clogged. What could she say? The man had a point.

She stood, offering him her hand. Ignoring the gesture, he averted his gaze. "Miss, I must insist you go at once and do not return until you are properly attired."

With a gasp, Kathleen realized she was in her nightgown. No dressing gown or house shoes—she'd been too afraid to remember either.

"Oh, my. I am so sorry. Of course. I'll just go and get dressed."

Not until she had changed into her gown and hooked her boots did she realize the irony of Mr. Carpenter scolding her about her appearance. She grinned as she headed back into the schoolroom.

Warmth met her from the fire Mr. Carpenter had built in the stove.

"Why, Mr. Carpenter. Thank you."

"You are most welcome. The desk was beyond repair, I'm afraid."

"I see." She gathered her courage and took a step closer to him. "May I ask why you came to the school at such an hour?"

He looked away. "I beg your pardon, miss. I succumbed to my weakness and visited the saloon."

Kathleen's eyes widened. "Well, you should be ashamed

of yourself. But that doesn't explain your presence here."

He shrugged. "The wind was extremely cold, and it was snowing so hard I could scarcely see where I was going. I knew I couldn't make it home, so I came here."

"Oh, it snowed? I best clear a path for the children."

"Don't bother. No one will be coming today."

"What do you mean? It's Tuesday. Of course they'll be here. It's a school day."

"Look outside."

Crossing to the window, Kathleen peeked through a circle Mr. Carpenter had wiped in the frosted glass. "Oh, my. I'm afraid you're right." Not only was the ground covered but heavy snow still fell from the sky.

"Naturally."

With a sinking—and slightly nauseated—stomach, Kathleen realized one more thing: If the children couldn't come to school, Mr. Carpenter couldn't leave.

By noon, the stench was beginning to waft into Kathleen's own living quarters, and she'd had all she could take. The ham she'd sliced for lunch sizzled in the skillet, the smell turning her stomach.

She tossed aside her book and flung open the door. "Mr. Carpenter, we need to talk."

He sat in *her* chair holding *her* book in his dirt-caked hands.

"Yes, miss?"

Her courage faltered, then revived as she thought ahead to the possibility of days and days with this man. "I haven't all day, Miss Johnson. I would like to get back to this perfectly delightful book." Kathleen recognized Edgar Allen Poe's name on the spine and rolled her eyes. She shook herself to get back to the matter at hand.

"Mr. Carpenter, I—I am afraid I must ask you—no, I must insist that you. . ."

He frowned. "Yes?"

"Sir, I beg of you to fill the tub and take a bath."

His eyes sparked as he jumped to his feet. "What?"

Kathleen shrank back from his anger.

"What right have you to insult me, young lady?" He glared down at her.

"I—I meant no insult."

He seemed not to have heard. "I was born and bred in Boston, the son of a wealthy merchant. I attended the finest schools and served as a schoolmaster in this very town until the war." He banged his fist on her desk, and Kathleen jumped, tears filling her eyes. "I am entitled to respect. I *will* be treated with decency!"

Fearing the wild fury in his eyes, she turned and fled the room. Once she was safely inside her quarters, she leaned against her closed door and willed her racing heart to return to a normal beat. Fat tears rolled down her cheeks. How could she have been so insensitive? From their first encounter, she had known that beneath Mr. Carpenter's exterior was a great man. She couldn't begin to fathom why on earth he would choose to live as he did, but wasn't she called to love him regardless? Would Christ have insisted he take a bath without taking the time to have a proper conversation?

Dear Lord, You brought Mr. Carpenter stumbling into the schoolroom as a blizzard roared. You knew we'd be trapped together, and You know how vile he smells. Please give me Your grace, compassion, and love for the man.

She walked to the stove and removed the slightly burned slices of ham from the skillet. She brewed a pot of strong coffee. When it was finished, she poured two mugs full, piled ham between two slices of bread, and returned to the school.

Mr. Carpenter sat in her chair, reading as before. He didn't look up. "I'd like to apologize, sir."

Still no response. Kathleen set the mug and plate before him on her desk. She took a gulp of her own coffee and nearly choked as it scorched her throat. "B—be careful. The coffee's hot."

He glanced up at her, curiosity in his eyes.

There. At least he was responsive. She began again. "I

had no right to speak to you as I did. You are a full-grown man of more intelligence than anyone I know, and you have the right to decide whether or not to bathe."

With a grunt, he eyed the sandwich and mug, then turned his attention back to his book.

Heat flooded Kathleen's face. "Well, I guess I'll. . .I guess you don't want company. I can drink my coffee back in my room." Turning, she swallowed back her humiliation.

"Wait, miss."

She turned back. "Yes, sir?"

"You brought only a cup of coffee for yourself. Are you not eating?"

So heavy was the stench, her stomach revolted against the thought. "Uh, no. I'm not very hungry."

He scrutinized her a moment, nodded, and then returned his attention to the book. Feeling dismissed, Kathleen returned to her quarters and picked up her knitting. Her lonely evenings had afforded her plenty of time to stockpile knitted gifts for her family and friends. Now she was determined to knit a stocking cap for each boy in her class and a scarf for each girl—something for them to remember her by when she went back home.

She had just finished another scarf when a knock at her door nearly sent her through the roof.

Mr. Carpenter handed her the mug and plate.

"Thank you kindly for your generosity," he said regally. "Now if I may trouble you once more."

"Of course. What can I do for you?"

"I'd very much appreciate the use of a pot with which to collect snow. And the wash tub. And one more thing. Might I trouble you for a blanket to wrap around myself while my clothes are drying?"

Kathleen collected the items he requested and threw in a chunk of lye soap.

"Thank you." He gave her a stern glance. "You must not enter the schoolroom until I return your items. I'm not entirely sure this is appropriate as it is. But for the sake of your appetite, I see no alternative."

Heat scorched her face and neck. "Of course."

She spent the afternoon listening to the door opening and closing more times than she could count as presumably Mr. Carpenter crammed pot after pot with snow to melt and warm on the stove. Thumps and sloshes were her music while she filled another pot with chunks of meat and canned vegetables—the Trumans' latest contribution to her welfare. She whiled away the afternoon, reading off and on, knitting, checking her pot frequently, and watching the clock. Curiosity nearly overwhelmed her at the thought of what Mr. Carpenter would look like absent the grime, though she was highly dubious as to whether he could successfully remove years of dirt.

The sun had set, and the stew filled the room with a tantalizing and most welcome aroma by the time Mr. Carpenter knocked on the door once more.

Kathleen gasped at the sight of him. He handed her the pot. "I apologize for not returning the rest of your items, Miss. The blanket you so generously supplied is soaking in the tub. And the soap is. . .well, I was forced to use the entire block."

"Oh, Mr. Carpenter. You look wonderful!" And she meant it. His skin, though red where he'd obviously scrubbed and scrubbed, was devoid of dirt. His gray hair hung to his shoulders, thick, with just a touch of wave. His clothes, though ragged and damp, were clean. She couldn't help the tears filling her eyes, and she quickly looked away, so as not to humiliate either of them.

"Won't you come inside and join me for supper, Mr. Carpenter?"

"Now, Miss Johnson. Have you no sense of propriety? Bad enough we must share two rooms. A grown man does not enter a young lady's sleeping quarters."

"Of course. M—may I join you for supper in the school?"

He scowled but gave a jerky nod. "Under the cir-cumstances, I believe that would be acceptable. But only because I am old enough to be your grandfather."

Kathleen beamed at him. "I'll dish up our supper and bring it in there lickety-split."

He turned away and headed away from her door, but Kathleen heard him mumbling, "Lickety-split. It's no wonder children today have such an appalling vocabulary when their teachers use such common speech."

She grinned as she filled their bowls. Who would have thought two unlikely people stranded together in a blizzard would turn out to be such a blessing?

Chapter 8

The blizzard stranded Mr. Carpenter in the schoolhouse for three days. During that time, Kathleen learned a great deal about the man. The torments of war had caused him to retreat into a shell. By the time he had come to his senses, he'd lost all credibility with the town. He sank into despair. Even before her death, his wife had grown so cold, life was nearly unbearable. Mr. Carpenter bore all the blame himself.

One thing she knew for sure: Mr. Carpenter's love of teaching was nothing less than a holy calling. He adored sharing knowledge. Kathleen had made up her mind to discuss his placement as the town schoolteacher next term. She felt certain if the school board spent time with him they would see him as she did—particularly if he resisted the urge to allow himself to go without bathing and abstained from even an occasional visit to the saloon.

By breakfast time on day four, Kathleen and Mr. Carpenter had pretty much run out of things to talk about, so it was with great relief that Kathleen responded to a knock on her door just as she returned the dishes to her quarters.

Mary and Josh stood outside. At least two feet of snow blanketed the area, with drifts as tall as Flora in some places.

"Mary! Josh! Come in. I'm so glad to see you."

Mary grinned, her face red from the cold. She stomped over to the stove and held out her large, rough hands. "Thought ya might be gettin' powerful lonesome."

Kathleen turned to Josh and smiled. "What are you doing in town?"

He smiled back, but his eyes held a serious look that made Kathleen want to run away, to hide from the temptation of falling in love with Josh Truman. It would be so easy to do just that. His kindness and humor drew her, and she'd never known a man to be so self-assured and yet vulnerable, as when he'd professed to having feelings for her so soon after they met. Josh was a rare man, and she knew someday he was going to make a woman very happy. She was almost jealous of whomever that woman would be.

"I hooked the team up to the cutter."

Mary harrumphed. "Rode those horses too fast, if you ask me. Downright dangerous."

Josh grinned, and Kathleen couldn't help but return it. "Sounds wonderful," she said.

"How would you like to go for a ride? I imagine you're just about crazy being cooped up for three full days all by yourself."

A knock sounded on the door between her quarters and the schoolroom just as she was going to explain about Mr. Carpenter. "Miss Johnson? Is everything quite all right in there? I thought I heard voices."

"Who in the. . . ?" Mary flung the door open. Mr. Carpenter gave a little scream and jumped back, fists up ready to defend himself.

Undaunted, Mary advanced. "Who are you? Whaddarya doin' in the schoolhouse, and what have you done to our little girl?"

Mr. Carpenter gaped. "I beg your pardon? I wouldn't lay one finger on that child, and I highly resent the implication."

Mary squinted and peered closer. "Myles?"

"Most certainly. Who else would I be?"

"Well, I'll be. . ."

Kathleen stepped between the two. "Mr. Carpenter

came into the schoolroom to get warm just before the blizzard hit. He graciously accepted my invitation to sleep in the school and has been a godsend. If I had not had his stimulating conversation these three days, I would be stark raving mad."

"Well, I'll be. . ." Mary stared at him. "I sure did forgit you was such a good-lookin' fellow, Myles." She glanced back at Kathleen. "How'd ya ever talk 'im into takin' a bath?"

"Why, Mary!"

"Sorry. But we been stayin' upwind from this fellow for years, and here he is in the middle of a snowstorm, smellin' like a dandy. I never would have believed it."

"For your information, Mr. Carpenter asked me for the loan of all things necessary to accomplish a bath, and I merely handed them over and stayed out of his way. The decision was entirely his."

Josh joined the three of them in the school. "You two stayed together for three days?"

Mr. Carpenter drew himself up with all the dignity he could muster considering his scarlet face—compliments of Mary's loose tongue. "We most certainly did *not* stay together. Miss Johnson stayed in her quarters behind closed doors, and I, a man old enough to be her grandfather, stayed as far back from her door as possible. However, if you feel she has been compromised, I will do my duty and marry her properly, lest her name and reputation be tarnished."

Kathleen gasped as horror tingled between her shoulder blades. Josh placed an arm about her and pulled her away from Mr. Carpenter. Mary scowled. "For pity's sake. That girl ain't been compromised. Now if it had been young Josh on the other side of that door 'stead of you, old man, we might have something to talk about. 'Sides, when this town gets a load of you in your new clean state, there ain't gonna be no other topic of discussion."

Mr. Carpenter looked as relieved as Kathleen felt at the cancellation of possible nuptials. Still drawn into the circle of his arm, Kathleen turned to Josh. Her face was inches from his, and she could feel his breath warm on her face. She swallowed hard in an attempt to compose herself and stepped out of his embrace. "Would you mind giving Mr. Carpenter a ride home in your cutter? He can't walk in this snow."

"I'd be happy to." Josh smiled—the gentle, intimate sort of smile reserved for a man in love. He stole her breath away, and she felt the heat rush to her cheeks.

"Thank you," she whispered.

"Yes, thank you." Mr. Carpenter's voice held just a touch of amusement. The first hint of humor Kathleen had ever detected in the man.

Josh broke eye contact and shifted his gaze to the former schoolmaster. "I'll wait while you get your coat."

The older gentleman cleared his throat. "I am quite ready when you are."

"You're crazy as a loon," Mary said. "It's at least ten below out there. Where's that army coat you been wearin' since '65?"

"The coat has been properly destroyed, as it should have been years ago."

Kathleen realized now what he'd been doing when he built a bonfire during a letup in the falling snow on the second day of their confinement. She walked to her quarters and hesitated only a moment before she peeled back her quilt. She folded it, then hugged it to her chest. As she walked back to the schoolroom, her mind argued with her nostalgic heart. Could she truly bear to part with her quilt? Perhaps Mr. Carpenter could simply cover with it on the way home and then give it back.

As soon as the thought came, she rejected it. In all likelihood, his blankets at home were as filthy as the coat had been. A new quilt would remind him of the dignity he'd acquired during the past three days and possibly discourage him from going back to his old ways. She had other blankets. But she wanted him to have something special to mark what she hoped was a new beginning.

A sudden image flashed across her mind of the beautiful quilt layered in grime. She shook the troubling thought away as quickly as it had come. She was only responsible to be generous. It wasn't up to her to judge what a person did with her gift. She had only to give it cheerfully as unto the Lord.

Mr. Carpenter's brow furrowed when she handed it to him and mentioned it was his to keep. "I'd like you to have this as a token of my appreciation for keeping me company during the storms. God knew I needed you here. I would have been petrified alone."

Tears misted in his eyes. Reaching forward, he cupped her cheek in his palm as though caressing a beloved child. "It is I who needed you, dear child. You have aptly spoken, in that God sent me here, but it is I who shall forever be grateful."

Impulsively, Kathleen hugged him. He patted her back awkwardly. Miss Bilge blew her nose loudly. "Well, if that ain't the nicest thing. . .well, I just don't know what is."

Josh grabbed Kathleen's hand and squeezed it. He, too, seemed moved by the scene, and Kathleen could almost feel God's stamp of approval as though He had put a period on a well-constructed sentence.

Mr. Carpenter glanced at Josh. "If you are ready, I must be going, young man. My home needs considerable work, and I'd like to get to it."

"Yes, sir. I'm ready when you are." Josh squeezed her hand again. "I'll be back later to take you home, Miss Bilge. And to take you for that ride," he said, his gaze settling on Kathleen in a way that made her pulse leap.

When the men had left, Mary Bilge stared at Kathleen for a long second. "That offer to save me a seat in church still standin'?"

"Of course, Mary!"

She moved her head in a jerky nod. "I guess iffen the Almighty can change a fellow like Myles, there might just be hope for me after all."

Kathleen's lips curved into a smile, and delight rose in her chest. *Oh, Lord, Your ways truly are so much greater than mine.*

School remained closed for the rest of the week, and each day Josh arrived by noon to take Kathleen for a sleigh ride. On Saturday she packed a picnic lunch. They sat together under a warm lap blanket in the cutter. The sun's rays shimmered across the frozen lake and danced off the icicles hanging from the barren tree branches.

"I'm sorry we missed the November dance." Josh's voice broke a long silence. Each knew this would be their last sleigh ride for a while as school would be back in session on Monday. The mood between them had been somewhat subdued.

"I don't suppose they'll reschedule since the blizzard caused it to be canceled."

Josh shook his head. "Pa said the recreation committee decided two failed attempts were enough, and God must not want it to go on this year for some reason."

Disappointment crept over Kathleen. "I would have enjoyed dancing a waltz with you before I go home, Josh Truman." She tried to keep her voice light, but even she could hear the false gaiety.

He stretched his arm across the top of the seat and cupped her shoulder, pulling her to him. "I would have enjoyed a waltz, too, Kathleen Johnson."

As his face grew closer, Kathleen fought a battle inside. As much as she craved his embrace, she knew it wasn't fair to either of them. She placed her palm against his chest and pushed slightly. "Josh, please. I've already told you that I have to go home in three weeks. Don't make me take the memory of your kiss with me. If I do, how will I ever fall in love with a man in Rosewood?"

A plethora of emotions seemed to cross his face as

though he struggled with his next course of action. Finally, he squeezed her shoulder and released her. Kathleen struggled against the feelings rising in her. All the emotions she'd felt over the past few weeks came to the surface, and tears pricked her eyes.

"Ah, Kat, don't cry."

"Kat?" Only those nearest and dearest to her had ever called her by her pet name.

"You don't like it? Kat suits you so well."

She smiled without elaborating. "I like it." Especially when it came from his lips.

As though reading her thoughts, he raised her gloved hand to his mouth. He kissed each finger, then pressed her palm to his cheek. He closed his eyes. "I want to remember this moment."

"W—we have three weeks. . . ."

"My heart can't take being alone with you and knowing you'll never be mine. Every time I'm with you, I fall deeper in love."

Oh, how she knew what he meant. But it would be so lonely without him for the next three weeks. The last day of school was only one week before Christmas. Then she'd go home and never see Josh again.

That night as she lay in bed listening to the sound of the mice scratching inside the walls, Kathleen remembered her brother's words to her. "Kat, don't make the same mistake I did. You might find that you don't want to stay in Rosewood forever."

Not stay in Rosewood? The thought had never occurred to her. Not in a million years. But now. . .

Was it possible?

Chapter 9

The next weeks moved frighteningly fast but at the same time crept along. Fast because Kathleen was busy with last-of-term grading and Christmas play practice. Slow because her sleep-lessness had returned. She tossed and turned at night, her mind racing over and over with scenes from the moments she had shared with Josh. She had seen very little of him since the day at the lake, and she missed him. No longer did she lie awake weeping for her family in Rosewood, though she still longed to see them, as well. Now she wept for Josh. Precious Josh. Josh, who would never belong to her.

The night of the Christmas play arrived with a chill in the air and a dampness that caused the old-timers to pre-dict a blizzard was coming. There hadn't been one flake of snow since the last blizzard, and everyone laughed off the predictions.

The children buzzed with excitement. Kathleen pulled a visibly nervous Andrew Coon aside.

"You're going to be wonderful, Andrew. Thank you for being our Joseph."

The teen had been a model student since the encounter with Mr. Carpenter and had even taken the initiative with the other unruly children. He'd become another gift from God. "My pa came. Said it was about time I did somethin' he could be proud of."

Andrew tried so hard to please the man—to make him proud.

She patted his shoulder. "We're about to start. Are you ready?"

"Yes, ma'am."

Kathleen smiled and moved back to the front of the room.

"Good evening, ladies and gentleman," she said, smiling at the crowd. A few returning smiles warmed her. Mr. and Mrs. Truman; the pastor and his wife; Mary Bilge, who sat beaming next to Myles. Much to the shock of the town, Myles had done an almost instant about-face and had stayed clean against dire predictions. He hadn't missed a church service, nor had Mary Bilge, and they'd recently taken up courting. Two more unlikely people Kathleen couldn't imagine, but according to Mary, he was teaching her etiquette and proper speech, and she was teaching him to laugh. Perhaps God had sent two lonely souls to one another.

Kathleen's gaze landed on Josh standing in the back of the schoolroom, leaning against the wall. Her pulse quickened at his crooked smile. But there was no time to ponder her feelings; she had a play to oversee. "I would like to introduce our narrator for the evening—a truly brilliant man with a gift for literature—Mr. Myles Carpenter."

He seemed ill at ease as he stood and came to the front. When the idea had occurred to Kathleen that Mr. Carpenter's beautiful deep voice and eloquence of speech would make him the perfect narrator, she'd approached him with caution. She needn't have worried. He agreed to her request without question, and she had grown to love him more each day. At Kathleen's encouragement, he often showed up during afternoon sessions and read portions from Shakespeare, Charles Dickens, Tennyson, and even Edgar Allan Poe. The children adored him, and he rarely had occasion to reprimand.

"Glory to God in the highest, and on earth peace, goodwill toward men." Kathleen came back to the present as Myles's voice accentuated the words. She peeked at the audience to see if they were equally affected. The spell-bound looks on their faces convinced her that Myles had a captive audience.

Not a dry eye remained as he finished the story with Simeon and Anna's blessing over the baby Jesus.

Mary and Joseph smiled at each other and held their "baby," which was actually made of straw.

"And that, my friends," Myles said, his voice shaking with awe, "concludes the wonderful story of the birth of our dear Lord."

For a long few seconds, no one moved, then slowly people began to clap, then stand. Barely a dry eye remained. Kathleen had never been so moved by a Christmas play.

The pastor shook her hand afterward. "I'm so pleased by all you've accomplished these past two months, Miss Johnson. Can't we convince you to stay on another term?"

As much as she'd considered staying for Josh, the thought of teaching left her cold. "These children are wonderful, as is Coon's Hollow, Pastor, but I'm afraid teaching isn't the profession for me."

"But you've done so well."

"Pastor, may I be honest?"

He grinned. "I wouldn't have it any other way."

She returned his smile. "Of course you wouldn't. I would like to suggest that you hire Myles to teach."

Alarm shone in his eyes. "Myles?"

"The children are thriving because of his influence in my classroom. Myles comes most afternoons. The students adore him. I don't believe you'd be sorry."

"Well, I certainly never would have thought of him, but perhaps you're right. I will look into it."

"Thank you, sir."

The pastor smiled again and looked over her shoulder. Instinctively, Kathleen turned. Her pulse thumped in her throat. "Hi, Josh."

"Hi, Kat." His gaze perused her face. "Your play was very nice."

"Thank you. I can't take much credit."

They stood at a loss for words. Finally, Josh broke the silence.

"You're leaving tomorrow?"

She nodded, gloom descending. "My train leaves at ten in the morning. Will you come see me off?"

"Won't you change your mind? Say you'll come back after Christmas and marry me."

"Oh, Josh, my mother would be so hurt. My family stays in Rosewood. I just can't go against that."

"Then you're robbing yourself of happiness with the man you love."

He spun around and stomped away, leaving Kathleen's

heart shattered on the wooden floor.

With aching heart, Josh watched the train pull away from the station. He expelled a heavy sigh. *Well, Lord. That's that, I guess. I tried. I felt sure she was the one for me.*

The snow was falling with more force, and he turned his collar up to ward off the icy blast of wind. A sliver of unease crept through him as the wind howled. With a frown, he nudged Shasta. Rather than turning and heading home, he found himself in front of the school almost without memory of how he'd gotten there.

His memory played in his head like a picture book. His first sight of Kathleen's blue eyes and sweet dimple. The musical sound of her laughter. Her kindness to Mary and to Mr. Carpenter. There would never be another girl like Kathleen Johnson.

He went home and moped for a good four hours while the snow continued to blanket the area. Alarm seized him when Pa entered the barn near suppertime.

"What's wrong, Pa?"

"I'm not sure, but I'm afraid the train to Rosewood might be in trouble."

Josh's mouth went dry. "What makes you think that?" he choked out.

"A rider came into town. Said it's been snowing that direction for a full day longer than we've had it. Snow's piling up. If it's over the track, the train could be in for some problems. I figured you'd want to know."

Josh had already moved into gear. He grabbed a harness and headed for the horse stalls.

"Josh!" As chaos and panic struck the passengers inside the tipping train, his was the only name Kathleen could remember, and she screamed it over and over as she fell. It all happened so fast that it took awhile for Kathleen to realize the train had derailed and she was falling. Pain hammered her right shoulder. And hip. When the car finally stopped moving and groaning, she tried to stand, but the shape of the train and the benches was too awkward for her to walk on with unsteady legs. So she crawled.

Her head felt light, as though she might faint. Oh, how she'd give anything if Josh were with her right now.

"Is everyone all right?"

The sound came from somewhere outside the train. It couldn't be Josh. He was back in Coon's Hollow. "I'm going to need someone to go to the lever and open the door. I can't get it open from out here." There was no mistaking the sound of that voice.

"Josh? Josh? Is that you?"

"Kathleen? Honey, are you all right?"

"I think so. Just a little bruised."

"Oh, thank God. Can you get to the lever?"

"I'm almost there."

In a moment, she opened the door and felt herself being pulled up. He sat on the side of the train and gathered her in his arms. "My love. Are you sure you're all right?"

"I am now."

"Is everyone all right down there?"

"I don't know. I think so."

He called down, and when no one reported anything but minor injuries, he promised they would send help back.

Since they were several hours closer to Rosewood than Coon's Hollow, Josh turned his team toward Kathleen's hometown. After they spoke with the mayor about the train, Josh headed toward Kathleen's house, then stopped before they got there.

"Kathleen." He looked into her eyes, and the intensity of his gaze nearly clouded her senses. "I can't let you go."

Tears filled her eyes. "I know. I feel the same way. But my family. That is. . .my mother especially. They expect us to stay in Rosewood."

"Sweetheart, I can't move here, if that's what you're thinking. I have a family, too, and my own squared-off piece of land that I've been clearing this winter."

"I know, Josh."

"I want to ask you something. I can't go all of my life knowing I didn't at least ask."

Kathleen closed her eyes, then opened them again.

Josh took her hand in his and pinned her with his gaze. "Kathleen, I've fallen in love with you. From the moment I saw you, I felt you were the girl for me. I want to ask you to be my wife. Will you marry me?"

"Oh, Josh." The negative response was on her lips, but she realized she couldn't say no. She just couldn't. She didn't even want to. "I will marry you."

His eyes widened. "You will?"

"Yes. I will."

He crushed her to him, taking her breath away. "Are you sure you can leave home?"

"Coon's Hollow is home now. I miss Mary and Myles, Flora and the boys, and even Andrew Coon. I want to go back and be a part of their lives."

"I'm so glad." He lowered his face, and this time Kathleen didn't resist. His mouth pressed against hers, soft and warm and filled with promise. Josh pulled away and looked deeply into her eyes. "I love you."

"I love you, too, Josh."

When his lips descended, Kathleen knew without a doubt that she'd finally come home.

Epilogue

Christmas morning

A bel Coon sneered at the two of them.

"Don't worry about him, Josh," said his wife of three days. "We'll beat him by a mile."

After meeting Kathleen's parents, Josh had asked for her father's permission to marry her. Kathleen had stood strong against her mother's protests, and Josh had returned to Coon's Hollow with Kathleen as his wife.

This beautiful Christmas morning had dawned bright, a perfect day for the Coon's Hollow Christmas sleigh ride—and Josh and Abel's yearly race. Josh hadn't lost one yet, and he'd informed Kathleen he didn't intend to start now.

She nestled in beside him, feeling the muscles in his arms tighten with anticipation.

The gun sounded, and they were off, each cutter sliding through the snow. After a minute, Josh got a margin of a lead and knew the race was all but over. Sandy and Chester weren't going to let Abel Coon win now that they'd had a taste of being ahead. The horses were more competitive than he was.

"Oh, Josh. There's our lake."

Trying to stay focused on the race, Josh didn't comment.

"Our lake. Where you almost kissed me. Where we admitted our feelings for the first time."

With a sigh, Josh slowed the cutter. Abel dashed ahead, a grin splitting his face.

"What on earth are you doing, Josh Truman?"

"I'm letting Abel have the race." He nudged the horses to the right and pulled them to a stop in front of the lake. The frozen crystals shimmered.

"But, Josh, you always beat Abel."

"Some things are just more important. Like a man kissing his wife next to a beautiful frozen lake."

There was no time for her to respond as he pulled her close. He kissed her thoroughly until all thoughts of

Abel Coon's first-place finish in the race fled from Kathleen's mind.

"Let's go home," he said.

Kathleen nodded. "Yes, let's go home."

Tracey V. Bateman lives with her husband and four children in southwest Missouri. She believes in a strong church family relationship and sings on the worship team. Serving as vice president of American Christian Romance Writers gives Tracey the opportunity to help new writers work toward their writing goals. She believes she is living proof that all things are possible for anyone who believes, and she happily encourages those who will listen to dream big and see where God will take them.

To learn more about Tracey, visit her Web site, www.traceybateman.com. Her e-mail address is tvbateman@aol.com.

A Letter to Our Readers

Dear Readers:

In order that we might better contribute to your reading enjoyment, we would appreciate your taking a few minutes to respond to the following questions. When completed, please return to the following: Fiction Editor, Barbour Publishing, Inc., P.O. Box 719, Uhrichsville, OH 44683.

1. Did you enjoy reading *A Christmas Sleigh Ride?*
   ❑ Very much—I would like to see more books like this.
   ❑ Moderately—I would have enjoyed it more if _____
   _____
   _____

2. What influenced your decision to purchase this book?
   (Check those that apply.)
   ❑ Cover   ❑ Back cover copy   ❑ Title   ❑ Price
   ❑ Friends   ❑ Publicity   ❑ Other

3. Which story was your favorite?
   ❑ *Colder Than Ice*   ❑ *Take Me Home*

4. Please check your age range:
   ❑ Under 18   ❑ 18–24   ❑ 25–34
   ❑ 35–45   ❑ 46–55   ❑ Over 55

5. How many hours per week do you read? _____

Name _____

Occupation _____

Address _____

City _____ State _____ Zip _____

E-mail _____

JHEARTSONG ❤ PRESENTS

Love Stories
Are Rated G!

That's for godly, gratifying, and of course, great! If you love a thrilling love story but don't appreciate the sordidness of some popular paperback romances, **Heartsong Presents** is for you. In fact, **Heartsong Presents** is the premiere inspirational romance book club featuring love stories where Christian faith is the primary ingredient in a marriage relationship.

Sign up today to receive your first set of four, never-before-published Christian romances. Send no money now; you will receive a bill with the first shipment. You may cancel at any time without obligation, and if you aren't completely satisfied with any selection, you may return the books for an immediate refund!

Imagine. . .four new romances every four weeks—two historical, two contemporary—with men and women like you who long to meet the one God has chosen as the love of their lives. . .all for the low price of **$10.99** postpaid.

To join, simply complete the coupon below and mail to the address provided. **Heartsong Presents** romances are rated G for another reason: They'll arrive Godspeed!

YES! Sign me up for Hearts ❤ng!

NEW MEMBERSHIPS WILL BE SHIPPED IMMEDIATELY!
Send no money now. We'll bill you only $10.99 postpaid with your first shipment of four books. Or for faster action, call toll free 1-800-847-8270.

NAME _____

ADDRESS _____

CITY _____ STATE_____ ZIP_____

MAIL TO: HEARTSONG PRESENTS, P.O. Box 721, Uhrichsville, Ohio 44683
or visit www.heartsongpresents.com